Be Not Weary in Well-Doing

Be Not Weary in Well-Doing

SARAH BELL

Copyright © 2015 by Sarah Bell.

Library of Congress Control Number:		2015917408
ISBN:	Hardcover	978-1-5144-1921-2
	Softcover	978-1-5144-1920-5
	eBook	978-1-5144-1919-9

All rights reserved. No part of this book may be reproduced or transmitted in any form or by any means, electronic or mechanical, including photocopying, recording, or by any information storage and retrieval system, without permission in writing from the copyright owner.

Any people depicted in stock imagery provided by Thinkstock are models, and such images are being used for illustrative purposes only. Certain stock imagery © Thinkstock.

Print information available on the last page.

Rev. date: 10/21/2015

To order additional copies of this book, contact:
Xlibris
1-888-795-4274
www.Xlibris.com
Orders@Xlibris.com
720060

CONTENTS

Epilogue..vii

Chapter 1 A Time for Every Season..................................1

Chapter 2 A Time to Heal, A Time to Build Up 25

Chapter 3 A Time to Break Down, A Time to Build Up..............50

Chapter 4 A Time to Plant Those Who Sew in Tears
Shall Reap in Joy 63

Chapter 5 A Time to Love..76

Chapter 6 A Time to Remember Precious Moments....................91

Chapter 7 A Time to Weep, A Time to Mourn 113

Chapter 8 A Time to Keep Silence, A Time to Speak 123

Chapter 9 A Time to Embrace, A Time to Refrain
from Embracing.. 135

Epilogue

A lot has happened since I wrote this book eighteen years ago. My son has a busy fulfilled life, and my daughter lives in town with two wonderful children, and I get to be very much part of their lives. My children's father passed away fifteen years ago and he is missed. It is always sweet to hear wee Noah talk about Grandpa Mike even though they never met.

Has my life been blessed since I wrote the book? Yes, so blessed. In fact, I often feel like the most blessed person in town. My kids are close. I live in a very beautiful, small community. I am part of a wonderful little church where people really love each other and truly function as a family. And, a very happy part of my life is that I now can make annual trips to Ireland to see the family that I love and miss so much.

Throughout this book I encourage you to put your children first – your time will come. And throughout this book I write often about wanting more time to knit. These days, I knit a lot and have my own knitting business. Better still, I get to teach knitting. My two favorite things to do.

I retired almost two years ago after almost forty-six years in nursing, and have never been busier, or happier. So, just want to share and encourage you once again. Be not weary in well doing. Devote quality time to those beautiful children. Your time will come

Chapter 1

A Time for Every Season

To everything, turn, turn, turn,
There is a Season, turn, turn, turn,
And a time for every purpose under Heaven.

There is a time for every season, and seventeen years ago, it was time to leave what I knew as my home. It was a decision that took years to make. I did not like divorce and was reluctant to become yet another California divorcee. Most of all, I was afraid. Earlier in my life, I had traveled a lot and had exciting adventures, all of which took courage. Why was I so afraid now? Because now I had two children whom I loved and adored, and my self-esteem was practically non-existent. I believed in very little and I certainly did not believe in myself.

All I knew was that I was supposed to go. My faith came and went like the waves as the tide comes in. I borrowed five hundred dollars from my sister in Ireland and left with eighty dollars in my pocket, I was six thousand miles from my family. My nine-month old baby had just been diagnosed with "failure to thrive" and I was underweight, and an emotional wreck.

This is not a sob story, yet, perhaps, the way many of us start the incredible task of raising children alone? Often we do not start from a great vantage point, but wearied already from what has been happening in the preceding years.

Raising well loved, healthy, children, is a great challenge for even two parents who are strong and love each other. Raising well loved, healthy, children as a single parent can be an overwhelming task. It does not just happen. It takes a lot of love and discipline, not just with our kids but with our selves also.

How can we raise children with good self-esteem when our own is so low? How can we teach our children about love when our own lives are full of anger, bitterness and unforgiveness? How can we be two parents to them and meet all of the financial needs? How can we provide for them and still share with them and give them the love they deserve?

It is truly awesome and so overwhelming. I remember those days. When children are little, we willingly put our dreams aside temporarily and many activities, which we enjoy, are often put on the back burner. Our lives are very busy. I used to say to myself, "One day I will write a book to encourage single moms." My heart feels for single moms. Does anyone truly know their plight if they have not had the opportunity of being a single parent? Perhaps not.

I am writing this book to encourage you. I made many mistakes but somewhere, somehow something worked and I have two wonderful kids who make me feel very proud to be their mother. To me, they are still very special. We had very little money but we had so much love. Together, we made it happen. We grew together, we worked together, we snuggled and read for hours together. Raising kids is like planting a garden. We sow the seeds and we water with lots of love. One day we reap what we have sown and we are blessed to see the wonderful adults our children have become.

I wrote this book to encourage you to be not weary in well-doing. Do not despair. Love your children and create a loving environment. Do not hesitate to put your dreams aside temporarily. Your time will come and it will be special because your own child may be your best support and encouragement.

Yes, it can be a lonely, overwhelming task and sometimes we cry from physical fatigue or emotional exhaustion, but our reward is worth every tear. One of the activities that I put on the back burner was writing but every now and again I seized the opportunity to put thoughts down on paper because it seemed to help. Last year I found this written prayer (chat) with the Lord. It was written about fifteen years ago when the kids were very little.

Be Not Weary in Well-Doing

It is tough Lord, it's so hard. My life I mean. There are times when I am so tired and exhausted that I cry. There is no end to the housework, financial problems, daycare problems. My days off are spent cleaning house. My evenings are spent making dinner, doing dishes, doing laundry, packing diaper bags and giving all I can to my kids.

Sometimes I feel so alone. There is no help. No one understands the endless work, the ceaseless demands. And sometimes I feel so sad because my children do not have a father close by. I'm hopeless at baseball. I can't be a father! "Lord, help me to enjoy baseball and football."

And Lord, sometimes I feel so lonely and so vulnerable. I dream of some wonderful man picking me up at 7:30 and taking me out to dinner. I would dress up and he would take me to a wonderful restaurant where we would eat delicious seafood. We would be waited on and wine and dine without interruptions like "Mom, come see." Instead we would listen to classical music and he would hold my hand across the table.

After dinner, we would walk by the ocean. (He would hang his jacket over my shoulders of course). Then we would go to his cabin where it is warm and quiet, except for Beethoven playing in the background. He would rekindle the fire. And then of course, he would tell me how much he liked being with me. What a dreamy evening we would have!

Oh Lord! be patient with my ramblings and meandering, my need to escape sometimes. We know that guys are pretty gun-shy around me. They watch what I go through. A normal hectic day in my life will scare any sane man away.

I love my children. I love the time I spend with them. What a blessing they are! It is tough Lord. And yes, many friends do not understand the pull of my heart. The commitment to these children. Help me to take one day at a time. Help me not be "weary in well doing." Who I am and what I do is molding the lives of these children.

I must be strong for them. They don't know the struggles, the dreams placed on the back burner, and they don't need to know. What they need to know now is that their mother loves them and that they are very, very special. They need the security; the routine. Most of all they need to know that the world is a good place to be and their opinions are valued and appreciated.

Lord, I am tired in body, mind and spirit. Help me not be weary in well doing. I know the reward will be great. Help me remember that it is not the quantity of time that I spend with them, but the quality of time.

Thank you for their works of "art" and "words of wisdom". Thank you for their hugs and kisses, requests for yet another story, and yes, even their sticky little hands and hand prints all over the window. Thank you for the physical and mental exhaustion. Thank you most of all that the three of us are together and know a life full of love and free of friction. It is a good life. It is good to be tired, fall into bed and rise in the morning to a fresh new day. A day filled with demands, children's drawings, and lots of hugs and kisses.

I may be tired, weak and vulnerable, but that is O.K. I know that the strength will be there for another new day. My heart is filled with anticipation. We are on a journey called Life. My children and myself together. Yes lord, I remember, "be not afraid"...

The Plight of the Single Parent

All across these United States of America, and unfortunately in other countries also, as the divorce rate continues to rise, there are single parents facing the challenge of raising children alone. What a sad state of affairs the family unit is becoming. Parents struggling alone, and children growing up with only one parent. Emotionally and physically, our plight is very real. Many of us are far from families who would help us. However, if we move to be close to family, we may be taking our children from the other parent who also wants to be with the children.

And what about our children's need to be able to see both parents? And what about those who do not even have contact with the other parent and have no financial support? And the children ask who their other parent is, and why they never come to visit as other childrens' parents do? What about the fact that we are only one person filling the role of two? Often we do the work of two people. Often we walk in two sets of moccasins in a given day. As sole bread winners, we cannot make as much money as two. We can work two jobs, but usually this defeats the purpose because we leave our kids for even more hours when what we really want is to be home with them and be part of their lives. Yet our children need food, clothing and a roof over their heads.

Yes, sometimes our hearts hurt, and often we have fears. Who is caring for our little ones while we earn a living? How will we ever pay these bills? Yes, it is overwhelming at times and I remember the stress and physical fatigue. There were nights when I cried from plain old exhaustion and possibly even despair. I was six thousand miles from home and could not return to Ireland because their father was in California. I wanted my kids to be able to see their dad.

As a nurse my job was quite demanding, especially considering that I was not in good shape emotionally, I had many concerns about day-care situations While I had to work. Financially, we struggled and I was a real worrier. I felt guilty about having to leave the kids and wanted nothing more than to spend time with them, they were so precious to me.

At first I did not experience loneliness. I was much too busy in "Survival Mode." There did come a time though when I did feel the need for love and emotional support. Life can be tough and very lonely for a single parent. We work hard, give so much love to our kids, deal with crises at work and home. But what about our own needs? Where do we go for love and support? I can only speak for myself here, but I love to be loved and I have a lot of love to give. I enjoy romance. There were times when it would have been special to snuggle up with someone and share the cares of the day. It would have been nice to have someone to lean on during those moments of weakness. Oh, the joys of being human.

I did have needs, but my children had needs also. Just as we are the product of our environment, so are our children. Children need a loving environment. Children become what they see. I had memories as a child. Did I want my children to grow up with similar memories and experience what I had experienced? We cannot protect children from everything in life, but we can, while they are little, provide them with a loving environment. That environment has a lot to do with the adults in our lives. I'm not saying that we should not go out on dates, or have relationships, but I do believe that we need to be very careful which adults and friends we invite into our home. Will this man respect our children and set a good example?

Often, significant others resent the time we spend with our kids and want to spend time with us alone. It is good for us to be alone with adults and go out for a nice evening. But all too often, unless it is a good relationship which adds to yours and your children's lives a relationship can interfere with the loving relationship that you have with your kids and add conflict to it. I did not want that to happen. My children had already experienced a divorce and had to adapt to new things in their lives. Dad lived over a hundred miles away and grandma had gone back to Ireland. The last thing these kids needed was another loss, upheaval or added conflict.

The most impressionable years in a child's life are from birth to six years. Patterns and behaviors are learned. Yesterday, when my daughter and I were talking about this, she reminded me, "Mom, kids get attached to their mother's boy-friend, and when it doesn't work out, they miss the person." She did go on to say that she had missed a friend when the relationship split up. She was about nine at the time. Our children are affected by our relationships with other adults. The people in our lives touch the lives of our children. Are they loving caring people?

Yes, I needed companionship just as much as my kids needed a loving environment. And yes, sometimes the woman in me wanted some TLC. I still feel that occasionally. Just this week I was thinking about how long it had been, and how nice it would be to go out on a date and be treated very special. But I learned something very special back in those days as a sometimes weary, sometimes alone single mom, and that is the importance of a support system. I had never heard of a support system back then, but it happened in my life.

I realize now that I just could not have made it without those wonderful people. It was difficult at first because I had a difficult time asking for help and still do. It is that old Irish pride and I was blessed with a double portion. In spite of my pride and unwillingness to ask for help, my support system was there. I had a few great friends at work, and it was a happy day when a friend invited me to her. What a great bunch of people. They took me in and loved me.

We all need love and support. We need to be with friends who love and protect us. Most of all, we do need to be able to share our cares and burdens. Sometimes we just need to talk. Maybe you do not have a loving little church to go to, but there are other support groups. If there is not a support group in your town, maybe you could start one.

Develop friendships with other single parents and share the load and encourage one another. It is so tough to be out there like the Lone Ranger. You are not alone. There are so many other single parents struggling as you are. They face the same dilemmas and carry the same burdens. Other single parents are tired and overwhelmed also. They need your input and support as much as you need theirs. Some single moms are struggling with "Teenager" problems, not knowing where to turn and feeling very helpless.

I wish that I could reach out and touch the lives of so many single parents who are struggling. I remember so well those early years and I still cry sometimes when I see others go through the same trials. But I cannot help everyone. All I can do is encourage you to, be not weary in well doing. It is a tough walk. Hang tough. Plant those seeds of love and watch the garden grow. Find supportive friends or a Support group who will offer love and encouragement.

I was especially blessed. My "support system" was my friends. My children, especially when they were very young, grew up around adults, most of whom loved and cared for them and had a positive effect on their lives. Many of those friends also protected me. I did have some relationships over the years, but I am glad even today that children came first. Glad, because now I have two wonderful children and I love the adults they are becoming.

I am not saying that friends and a support system will take the place of that special significant other. I do believe though, that having companionship and support may help us not to make poor decisions out of loneliness or neediness. Those poor decisions could negatively affect the lives of the children we so dearly love. And it is tough love. We may need love and affection but, believe it or not, our children need it even more.

Yes, I was especially blessed. My friends had "Love with legs."

Love with Legs

There is so much talk about love today. Every kind of love. Romantic love, unconditional love, parental love. I read a quote once, "It is easier to love humanity as a whole, than to love one's neighbor." It is sad but true. We talk about our concerns for starving children, cruelty, war, abuse and discrimination.

Many of us lament about the state of the world with all of its pain and sorrow. But, how do we reach out to a world, which hurts so much? Perhaps we can start by loving and helping those around us. Our children, parents, neighbors, the elderly amongst us and even the children of single parent families. And we can always remind ourselves that "love" is usually a verb, an action word.

Few of us are able to leave home and work with starving children or refugees, but many of us can reach out to those around us. It does not have to be in a dramatic way. Usually it is just a matter of seeing a need, and meeting it when it is within our power to do so.

Much of the time, talk of love is just that, talk. I fall into this trap myself. The other kind of love, the kind that motivates us to action, I call "love with legs."

My wish is that each single parent would know at least some of the "love with legs" whom I knew. Many of my friends were "love with legs" personified. This single mom did not do anything to deserve these wonderful friends. They were a gift from the Lord. I do not know why I was blessed with their friendship, but I can honestly say, I could 'not have made it without them. Oh, the kids and I would have survived, but their love was a huge part of the healing process that was to be ours over the years to come.

I was broken and in much need of healing. My self-esteem was as low as self-esteems can go. My heart was hurting and wounded, even though I did not feel it. Guess I was too numb to feel anything. How can a marriage end in disaster and those involved not be hurting? Is it possible? Even if the separation is a good move, there is still pain and disillusionment for most involved, like parents, grandparents and children. Unfortunately, we are too absorbed in our own pain and confusion to even think of the other party. They are probably going through the same thing.

Basically, I was in survival mode and had a huge undertaking ahead of me. I had two little children to raise in a foreign country, many miles from home and family. We arrived in Fort Bragg almost penniless. It was October and winters were cold on the coast. It was cold already.

Sometimes it is hard to believe how life was back then. We were alone and in much need of TLC. Thanks to those wonderful people, "love with legs" personified, that is exactly what we got.

Dorothea and Ivy

One of the most important days of my life was the day that I met Dorothea and Ivy. When I grow old, I want to be just like them.

I met them at church. One day they invited us home for lunch. I knew little about them except what I sensed in my heart. They were gentle, very strong, and very wise. That in its self was inviting.

I had every other weekend off and each Sunday off after church, I would take the kids to the beach - we loved that. But this day we went to lunch at the Dolphin house.

Dorothea and Ivy lived in a wonderful house out on the bluffs at Caspar. It was called the Dolphin house because of the sculpted dolphin, which protruded from the roof. The ocean could be seen from three sides of this two-storied house. I discovered that day that the Dolphin house was heaven and in it lived two angels who loved needy people like myself.

This home was paradise and these two angels lived their lives ministering to the needs of others. Lunch was a banquet. It seemed that everything was home-made or home-grown. Ivy was the gardener and both enjoyed preparing food. Being around these two ladies was "love." Their home was permeated with love, not because it was beautiful and rustic, but because even the walls had absorbed the love of the two souls who lived there.

I don't remember what happened that day during that wholesome lunch prepared by loving hands, but I do know that it was the beginning of years of healing long overdue in my life. There was no criticism and there were no "shoulds." Only be strong; be of good courage. Not in old fashioned words like that, but somehow that was the message imparted to me that day.

They loved Noah and Suzanne and we became their charges, but without any of the control that often comes with someone taking you under their wing. Very much the opposite.

They were like mothers, but they never mothered me. Nor were they judgmental. Theirs were words of love and encouragement. When I was weak, they helped me be strong. When I was falling apart, they supported me as I picked up the pieces. And best of all, they loved my children. Their love was so quiet and drawing that my children performed to the utmost, not because they had to, but because they loved Dorothea and Ivy and wanted to please them.

Dorothea was an artist, genteel and soft-spoken. A well educated lady who had done much in her life-time. Her purpose in life now was to serve the Lord, and that she did in quietness and humility. As an artist, she recognized and drew out the artistic side of these two children.

Dorothea lived a quiet peaceful life of service. She had the heart and soul of an artist, but her real love was intercessory prayer. She made silk batiks out of bees' wax and it was by selling these wonderful works of art that she supported herself. Her studio was an artist's delight. It was about 100 yards from her house. It was so adorable, about eight feet long and eight feet wide, designed after her home. From three sides of the studio she could see her beloved ocean. Each day she would walk over to her studio and work. And I know that those quiet hours of solitude were spent in prayer and meditation as she created her beautiful silk batiks.

And Ivy, I love you so much. Ivy was/is the gardener, the fisherwoman, "The old lady of the sea". She gardens, she cooks, she does wood-work. She loves to read and she loves her children and grandchildren. Her heart is bigger than her tiny body - it's huge. Her life is serene and full of love. What an incredible woman; what a joy it is to know her. Ivy, how did you turn out to be so beautiful and special? You have had such hard times in your life, yet there is no resentment or anger: only a great peace and a love that reaches out to those in need.

But Dorothea and Ivy did not just love us with words (that's why I am telling you about them). They were there in real and practical ways. They were "love with legs."

My life was happier with Dorothea and Ivy in it. There was so much growth necessary, but with their encouragement, I was able to at least practice the art of letting go. Yes, life was getting to be more fun. At that time we lived out in the country on a wooded acre. We named it "Happy Acre," because in spite of everything, we were happy. Now on this acre was a double-wide trailer, about 20 years old by this time. Only problem with our little home was that the roof leaked in the winter time and not just a wee bit. Did I mention that it rains a lot in Ft. Bragg? Yes, sir, it rains and it rains!

So, every year before rainy season started this writer would mend the roof with "Henry's." Every year I climbed up on the roof with a 5 gallon bucket of the gooey stuff. It even got to be a joke at work. But, guess who was up there by my side now? Of course, it was Ivy. We would spend a beautiful sunny Fall day "up on the roof," with "Henry." Now, when Ivy is working alongside, it isn't work anymore! Spend a day up on the roof with Ivy and "Henry" and you will know what I mean.

One year, the rain was so heavy that my driveway (fancy word for a dirt road) was a mass of huge muddy pot-holes. Now, there was free gravel for the taking at Albion. That's cool if one has good biceps, a strong back and a pick-up truck. Well, I had good biceps and a strong back, but no truck. Who shows up? You guessed it; Ivy with her little Toyota pick-up truck. Ivy to the rescue again!

At this time Ivy was about seventy, but had the energy of a twenty-five year old. So, off we went to Albion with our shovels. We went and we went till we were spent, but happy. The driveway was as good as new. Now friends could come visit without getting stuck in the mud. Even love with legs would have a difficult time wading through all of that mud.

Life with Ivy wasn't all work. In fact the best times with Ivy were spent out on the ocean in her little "Skiff." With the fishermen in town, she earned the title of "The old lady of the sea." She was fearless and full of wonderful fishing and sea stories.

It is difficult for me to accept that some children grow up, never having experienced going out fishing on the ocean in Ivy's little boat. I covet this great adventure for every little kid. Now Ivy does other kinds of fishing, but when the kids and I were with her, we fished for Sand-dabs. When you fish for Sand-dabs, you just couldn't go wrong and Ivy knew that.

Sand-dabs are flat little fish that live on the bottom of the ocean. Kids love them because they have two eyes on one side (they lie on the bottom of the ocean) and they are so easy to catch. We just threw in our lines with about three hooks on each line and Lo and behold, there were two or three Sand-dabs. The kids were ecstatic! And did I mention that they are delicious? What a day, out on the ocean with Ivy catching fish.

But the experience did not end there. What's the point of catching fish if you don't know how to clean them? Ivy had a bench under the deck at the Dolphin house just for cleaning fish. "If ya wanna eat 'em, ya gotta clean 'em," she used to say.

Then to top it all off, we had a fish supper with Dorothea and Ivy, with fresh spuds and greens. What a great day! What a wonderful life we had. I was glad that we had a large freezer to keep all that extra fish. My kids and I still love seafood. My son, who just turned 19, still enjoys fishing and that makes me very happy. Thanks to Ivy, in spite of being raised by a single mom, my son learned to fish.

Dorothea was in her 70's then also but that didn't prevent her from having "love with legs." My heart is so appreciative of these two women. I remember once that I didn't have day-care in the mornings, between the time I left for work and the kids went to school. Let's face it, I had to work. It was not an option. So every morning, Dorothea was knocking on my door at 6:30 in the morning. I left for work knowing that all was well. Dorothea made breakfast for the kids and drove them to school. It brings tears to my eyes when I think of this, because even though she was in her 70's, Dorothea did still have a schedule to adhere to. Thank you Dorothea from the bottom of my heart.

A Retreat - Rest for the Soul

I often hear mothers say that they need a break from the kids and I must admit that I didn't experience those feelings. My time with these children was so special.

In the court settlement, it was written that Noah would spend every other holiday with his father and Suzanne would stay at home. However, most holidays I sent the children to stay with their dad. As a nurse, I often worked holidays. And after all, holidays with their dad were so much fun. Their aunt and uncle had a mini farm and 43 acres of land to explore. Each year, the family would get together there. Noah and Suzanne would get together with their cousins the same age, and each year they would celebrate Christmas with a huge Christmas tree. They had a wonderful time.

Consequently, I spent many holidays alone. I tried to be positive. This was an opportunity to spend time alone and do things that I didn't usually have time to do. But it just wasn't like that. I missed the pitter-patter of their little feet and their hugs and requests.

Dorothea and Ivy used to say, "just come on over here Sarah," I can just hear you say, "Now, what kind of fun would that be? Spending time off with two older ladies?" Now that is a pretty reasonable response, but you didn't know these two ladies.

I'd leave work after a hectic day and retreat to the Dolphin house. And that's exactly what it was, a retreat. There was time to visit, read, just walk out on the bluffs, or climb down on the rocks and watch the sunset. Dinner would be simple and scrumptious. Again, home-grown and prepared by artists in the kitchen. Even conversation over dinner was sweet and dishes an act of love.

Dorothea and Ivy's evenings were quiet, the kind we single parents dream about in the future (the kind that I have now). Ivy would light the big wood-burning stove. By the stove there was a window seat, big enough for Ivy and myself. Dorothea sat in the rocking chair usually. Together we would gaze out the window at the ocean. Dorothea would often be knitting, Ivy reading and I was usually knitting or reading. But together we would watch the ocean or the flames in the fire. We would knit and we would read, our hearts knit together. Our own thoughts, prayers and aspirations inspired by the ever-changing flicker of light in the fire-place. Usually, conversation was sparse but precious. We didn't need to talk.

My bed-room down-stairs was a dream. It was rustic, full of books, yarn, and Dorothea's silk batiks. Better still, windows without curtains. I could see the stars and below, I could see the reflections of the moon, glimmering on the ocean. Best of all, I could hear the roar of the ocean, restless, yet full of serenity and peace. In the mornings, early as it was, that fairy-land room was full of light, and oh, that wonderful sound again. To me, there is no experience like this. To awaken fresh (lulled to sleep by the sound of waves) with sunlight flowing through window-panes and the sound of the ocean pounding on the rocks, saying, "Wake up, you lazy creatures. It's time to start living!" But alas, what is this I hear? A sound unfamiliar to me, yet so pleasant. Yes, that is definitely the sound of coffee perking, and oh! that wonderful aroma! Think I died and went to heaven.

And what else is that I hear? Some hustle and bustle and very definitely, sweet soft voices and some occasional chuckles. Half awake, delirious and euphoric, I would drag my thirty-six year old body out of bed and climb the stairs. Wait for it! I stand and watch as Dorothea and Ivy prepare for their morning exercise routine. O.K., shake your weary bones and join in the fun. Did I mention that it isn't quite six in the morning?

No, life at the Dolphin house was certainly not boring. And these were not two old ladies. Their lives were full and fun.

I read the book, "When I am an Old Lady I Shall Wear Purple." Dorothea loved purple; Dorothea loved color. We used to talk about color a lot. Back then, Dorothea was possibly the only one who knew the deep regret and disappointment that I was feeling from not having pursued a career in art. As I talked about it, I was able to forgive and let go. Oh, the sweet freedom of forgiveness. Dorothea encouraged me that one day I would have the opportunity to pursue the dreams in my life (she was right of course).

And so, we'd pick out all the hidden colors that made up those glorious sun-sets. Even the gray skies have color if you look for them.

Yes, days at the Dolphin house were a "retreat" indeed. Rest for the soul that can become so weary.

Dorothea's Banquet

Dorothea is gone now; gone from this world I mean. The last few years that we lived in Mendocino County, Dorothea developed heart failure. Worse still, she had allergic reactions to the drugs typically prescribed for heart-failure.

If her life was quiet before, it was more so now. She could not leave home much. In fact, she could not walk to her adored studio. Her life must have been more trying, but it certainly was not evidenced much to those around her. Her cup just kept bubbling over. Her increased solitude served only to make her love and grace grow.

We missed Dorothea and Ivy when we left Mendocino County. Dorothea could not travel far from home due to her condition and I had a shop which left me with little time to travel.

Then one day, Ivy brought Dorothea to Calistoga on a day trip. What a great day. I closed the shop and we went to lunch at the Italian restaurant across the street. Dorothea was tired, but did wait until Suzanne came to the shop after school. She was not able to wait until Noah came home.

Dorothea was able to rest during that beautiful ride home while Ivy drove. They stopped and enjoyed the flowers. Oh, that wonderful and wise lady. I think she knew that soon she would be going home. She just wanted to sit with Jesus at the Banquet table. She went home to that banquet table about six weeks after this-last trip. She and Ivy went to church on Christmas Eve. She was actually sharing in church and lifted her hands to praise the Lord. She collapsed and died. Maybe she raised her hands to greet Him because she saw Him coming.

Oh happy day, that Dorothea was spared the pain of a long terminal illness. I'm a nurse and know that death can be prolonged, and people suffer much in their bodies before they leave this world. I work in long-term care and spend many hours a week in Nursing Homes. Dorothea was spared it all. She was in her beloved Dolphin house, by her beloved ocean until she went to the Banquet. There is no better way. Thank you Lord for sparing our friend those long remaining painful years on this earth.

I miss Dorothea of course and I know that Ivy must miss her even more, but in our hearts we are glad that she is really home. And Dorothea, thank you for loving us so much. Wish you could see how different life is now for the three little lost children you helped so much. Life used to be so much more difficult. Guess there are still trials, but thanks to the love that you and Ivy gave us, we are so much stronger.

Ivy, I Love You

I mentioned that Dorothea loved purple. Well, Ivy loves blue. She loves the blue of the ocean and the blue of the sky. Perhaps this is why her eyes are so blue. She watches the sea and sky so much, her eyes absorb their color. If this was possible, it would happen to my friend Ivy. "The Gutsy Lady."

She has her own little home now, out in the woods, still near the ocean and close to family. She's a happy lovely lady. She still works outside, loves to sit by her big wood-stove and read, and she still goes fishing.

I talked to Ivy on the phone to-day and she's as busy as ever. She's taking care of a 94 year old sister, baby-sitting her grand-children while their mom recovers from knee surgery and storing the onions and garlic she grew this year. On top of all this, she still had time to go fishing for salmon - and of course she scored! The question is, why am I sitting here in this heat, when I could be fishing with the most wonderful lady in the world?

Ivy, I miss you. Will you please take Noah and me fishing again?

Jim and Bonnie

Jim and Bonnie, your love had legs like a centipede. I don't know why Jim and Bonnie were so kind to us, but I do know that their love made a huge difference in our lives.

Jim was our pastor, a sweet loving man. Bonnie was his wife, an artist and a decorator. She was a sweet loving lady. Both had huge smiles and very loving hearts. They did so many wonderful, beautiful acts of love for Noah, Suzanne and me. They preached love and they practiced it. They took us under their wings and protected us like mother hens.

"Love with legs" is an understatement for these two wonderful people. Bonnie knew that I loved to decorate also and that if I had the finances, I would love to turn the covered deck into a third bedroom. One day after work, the kids and I went home to find Bonnie finishing installing beautiful curtains. She had also painted a beautiful picture of little children.

Jim was busy with his tools on the covered deck, creating the third bedroom that I wanted so much. They were so talented and creative. They made our little home so cozy.

I especially remember one Thanksgiving. The children were with their dad and I was at home very sick. I was hungry, but too weak to make food. It was raining outside and very cold inside. I was so homesick and I missed the kids (after all, Thanksgiving is a time to be with family).

Usually I had wood split and moved indoors to dry, but for some reason that day, I had no dry wood. I went out in the rain and attempted to split wood, but gave up after splitting a few logs. I was shivering and my chest hurt with the cold air. I put my few wet logs in the wood-burning stove and attempted to light the fire. It smoked and died. I gave up and once again, huddled under my down quilt on the couch and shivered painfully.

All of a sudden, I heard a knock on the sliding glass doors in front of me, and there stood Jim and Bonnie. I was so surprised to see them. I was supposed to work that day, and had declined invitations for Thanksgiving dinner, including Jim and Bonnie's. I lived four miles off the main highway, so, why were they here? Bonnie gave me a hug and I saw Jim glance at the wet, smoking, flameless fire. They said, "Sarah, you rest."

I shivered and hot tears flowed freely, soaking my pillow. I was homesick, I missed my kids, I was sore. My whole body ached. Actually, I really don't know why I cried. Maybe, I just needed to cry. I huddled into the quilt, longing for the pain to go away.

In just a little while, Jim and Bonnie returned. Bonnie propped me up on the couch and served me a huge plate of Thanksgiving dinner. As I picked at the food, I watched Jim unload dry wood on to the covered deck (a lot of it) and start a roaring fire. Yes, I had a lot to be thankful for that Thanksgiving Day. Two more wonderful friends who had "love with legs."

These are just a couple of the things that Jim and Bonnie did for the kids and myself during the few years that they were in Ft. Bragg. They were like parents to me. Jim and Bonnie, I will never forget you. Your "love with legs" went a long way. l just hope that I can love others as you both loved me. I miss you both very much.

Mom

What a hard-working, determined woman my mother was. Back then in Ireland, a woman stayed at home with the kids. My mother had to be creative and believe me she was.

I know that it wasn't easy for her raising us alone, but she did what she had to do. Sometimes the best motto is to take care of what is in front of us. Most of the time it isn't what we have to do in life that wears us out, but our attitude as we do it.

I don't remember her complaining much. Really, she just did it. Raise us I mean. A few years back, she made a comment to me, "I don't know what fear is." I believe that she does know what fear is, but because of the dragons fought in her life-time, has learned that fear is just another battle. The dragon in our life is not the battle. Our own fear is the real battle. Finding the faith and courage to take on the dragon is the real battle.

My mom did not tell this to me with words. She told this to me with her life. She is an amazing lady. Her good old Irish dad told her often (he told the same thing to me), "There's no such word as can't." I think that my mom took him quite literally. Even now I can see her standing with her hands on her hips and eyeing a wall. My poor old dad probably ran a mile when he saw that look. Over the last fifteen years

I have lived with my mom for periods of time. I know now what that eye-balling the wall and hands on the hips means. "That wall has to go!" Now herein the United States walls are usually made of wood. Yes, you know what is ahead, don't you? Yes indeed, we are talking Ireland here. And of course we all know what walls are made of in Ireland, don't we? Good old Irish stone. To Mrs. Sheeran it made no difference, down came the wall!

Sometimes I have a little chuckle to myself (I just smile and smirk). It's during these times (and I'm sure you will identify with this), when our daughters are irritated with our little ways and subtly express their disapproval, i.e. "When I am an adult, I won't act like that." Why does this make me chuckle? Because I am so like my mother.

Many times I find myself standing with my hands on my hips, eye-balling something and I just have to laugh at myself. And I say to myself, "You wouldn't." Then I answer myself, "Yes, you would." And I do.

My sweet mother does not attack walls any more, and her daughter is learning to leave walls and large pieces of furniture right where they are, but it was this kind of determination that brought about my mother's success. I say success, not because of her wealth; she does not have that. I say success because she raised six great kids who love her dearly. She is surrounded by nineteen grandchildren who are now having their own children. I say success because she loves challenges and would still love to start her own business. I say success because she is afforded the opportunity to help care for her own mother who is almost one hundred years old.

Yes, my mom gave so much. She gave so much to me and she made so many sacrifices. Actually, out of all of her daughters, I was the one who caused her so much concern and grief. I was the rebellious one who left Ireland at twenty-one and wanted to try everything. I know that it hurt her deeply to watch as I made those wrong turns that would later cause grief and sorrow that required years of healing.

The wonderful thing is that families can heal together, and we did. We do. I watched her go through some trying times. Sometimes a parent hurts more than the child hurts. Because of a very undesirable incident which occurred while she was here in California, at the last minute, we were unable to go home to my little sister's wedding. My mom was devastated and so was my little sister.

In the years that followed my divorce, my children's passports were confiscated (they were born in the United States), so that I could not take them to Ireland. At one point my grandmother was ill and I wanted to take the children home to see her. I hired an attorney and went to court to request permission to take the children with me on a trip to Ireland. I even provided the court with proof that I owned property in California. The court denied the request. Mom and I were heart-broken.

Several years later my father had a stroke and I went home to see him. I was allowed to take one child with me but was required to leave the other child. Time does heal though, and faith is restored. There came a day when both children went home with me to Ireland. Oh happy day.

Those years were tough for my mother, but they are long gone. Can you believe that we are even able to laugh about those times now? We didn't laugh about it back then. We were two sad mamas. Now we are two happy mamas and probably better individuals because of those trials.

Those hard times made us very, very close. She felt so deeply for the kids and for me. She even sold her home in Ireland and gave the proceeds to me to buy the little home in which we were living. It was so difficult to accept that money from my mom (she raised us to be so independent). I did accept and we bought our little home which we named "Happy Acre." We spent seven wonderful years on that happy acre.

I especially remember our first year there. We had just arrived in Fort Bragg and our financial situation was pretty grim. My mom only planned on staying for a few weeks to help with the move, but stayed for the whole year and cared for the kids. Noah was three years old and Suzanne was only nine months old. I was on call at the local hospital. It was a small hospital and there was not much work sometimes. I was so concerned about finances and fretted constantly. My mom encouraged me often. "Sarah, trust the Lord. He won't let you and your wee family go hungry." And of course our needs were met, but I know that I almost drove her crazy with my constant fretting and complaining.

I learned so much that first year. Each day after work, I would go home to a clean little home and well-loved kids. I saw it so clearly, the importance of harmony in the home. Now I was the breadwinner. What a pleasure it must be for a man to go home to a clean, harmonious home, well loved, mellow children, and a loving friend.

That was my treat for a year. My mom made dinner every evening and I had to be pushy just to get doing the dishes. Mom was always saying, "No, you spend time with the kids and I'll do the dishes." Often, after the kids had been tucked in, we would spend time in front of the big wood-burning stove and knit (not to mention the chats and laughs we had and the tears that we would cry).

And did I say that my mom made dinner every evening? To this day, I don't know what my mom made dinner out of. Sometimes, to me that fridge seemed so empty, yet every evening we ate a hot scrumptious meal. I used to think that she was the widow in the Bible whose vessels were full every morning. And why not? We were widows in a sense and my mother had enough faith for both of us.

It was time to plant a big garden, and an Irish garden must have spuds. What happy days we spent out on our little "Happy Acre" in the woods with two little children working side by side.

For the two kids, the best treat was hot Irish Soda Bread made by their own Grandma. This treat was part of Grandma's extended visits. She would make the bread and butter it right off the griddle.

Sometimes she would even do some landscaping while I was at work. I would ask, "Mom, how did you do this without tools?" She would say, "Oh, I have my ways." Did the tools appear from above, the same as the food appeared to? I have no idea - even to this day.

Yes, it was a wonderful year, and I must not forget the little sweaters that she knit and sold to help make ends meet. What a great friend she was. She taught me through her own example, how to be strong and how to be resourceful. That is quite a gift to give to a daughter.

I will never be able to repay my mother for all that she did for us. I do not believe that it would be possible to do so. I only know that she loved us through some hard times and that she truly was "love with legs" and more.

Thank you mom for all that you taught me. I just pray that I have inherited at least a little of your courage, strength and determination (although I have given up knocking down walls and leave that to the experts).

A Friend in Need, is a Friend Indeed

It is a glorious Fall day outside. The sky is blue and the leaves on the trees are turning orange and falling to the ground. They have supplied us with beauty all summer, and now it is their time to rest. Yes, there is a time for every season. There is a time to walk through the valleys and there is a time to be blessed beyond words as we walk through those valleys. The trees may look bare and barren through the cold winter but in the spring, their branches will again be beautiful and bear fruit.

I share this part of my life with you now because we are considering the importance of friends and support systems in our lives. When the kids were little I had a poster that said, "If you want a friend, be a friend." Usually I do not have the time to be the friend I feel that I could be because my life is so busy working long hours and commuting a couple of hours a day. So, where the wonderful friends in my life come from I will possibly never know. Friends are special and they never cease to amaze me.

You see, several months ago I lost my job. It wasn't the first time. Last year, the same situation 'had occurred, and that is when I wrote most of this book. It was difficult financially last year, but somehow the money was always there as I realized a dream and wrote this book. This year was a bigger hardship though, because I had not quite recovered from being unemployed for three months last year and worst of all, I knew that this time, I would be true to myself and not go back to the same type of work.

Temporarily, I did lose my equilibrium. Yes, after almost twenty-eight years in nursing, I had nursing and management skills but I was so busy raising children and working that I did not take the time (or make the time) to develop other skills. My heart was sad and concerned. I had a daughter in her senior year at school. How would I meet her needs? I had worked years at work which I had come not to enjoy and tried to hang on until she had finished school. I knew though, that for the sake of my health and my sanity, I could not go back.

It was a tough time already financially. I was sharing a house with a friend who had to move. The rent was eleven hundred dollars a month, and the move itself had cost money. Needless to say, money ran out fast after I lost my job. Yes, I did fall apart at first. But for everything there is a season, and I believe that everything in our lives happens for a reason. What is it that I need to learn from this?

I have learned a lot over the last few months. I have learned how to be a checker at a busy grocery store and how to work in the produce department. I have learned how to work in a "Bed and Breakfast" and how to landscape a window front. I have learned more patience and that there is a lot we take for granted in life and we can survive with less. I have learned to a greater degree, that what we "put out" in life will return and be multiplied. Above all, I have learned that our needs will always be met, that the Lord never fails us and that it is a great gift in life to have friends who love us and really care. Yes, a person who has true friends is truly blessed.

And blessed I am today in the valley because of my wonderful friends. Again, even on this beautiful Fall day, the view is changing and so is the season. I am on the incline, climbing the gentle slope, and I do it with the help of my friends.

A Sunflower Smiled over the Fence

It was Sunday, and I was finally able to cry. In fact, I was at a birthday party in the hills and I cried all day. Early Monday morning I would give notice to vacate this home, which I had been enjoying so much. Tuesday morning I would return the car to the Dealership. And, "no," my daughter would not go to live with her Dad. She would stay with me and together we would go through this. Some things we need to go through and this too would pass. After all, I had great health, two wonderful kids and I did have my bike - my old stand-by.

So, I did cry and work on my attitude. I had started from scratch before and I could do it again. No, I did not want to move but we would find a little apartment close to the school and I could ride my bike to work. Yes, I might shed a few tears out of self-pity but tomorrow I would be strong and deal with reality. I survived the Party (thank God for sun-glasses) and went to pick up my bike. I just couldn't believe it. The bike was gone. Well, I can chuckle to myself now as I write but I didn't chuckle then. That was the straw that broke this camel's back. I walked home, in tears once again.

My daughter greeted me with "Mom, Terry is coming over with a gift from Reno." The last thing I needed right now was company, so I asked her to call back and cancel. She said, "Mom, this is very important." I sat out on the back deck and tried to get my act together but only cried more. Then through my tears I saw it. A big beautiful Sunflower in the neighbor's back yard was leaning over and smiling at me. Isn't it strange how sunsets and new-born baby's little finger nails and beautiful smiling Sunflowers remind us that everything will be all right. "Consider the Lilies of the field: They toil not, neither do they spin." What a big, gentle reminder. Yes Lord, I remember, "Be not afraid . . ."

I was to shed some more tears that evening, but they were not tears of sadness, they were tears of joy. You see, this beautiful friend walked into my living room with a great big smile on her face and handed to me two thousand dollars in cash. I still cry sometimes when I think about her act of kindness and the pleasure she had as she handed her gift to me. This is just one of the many Random acts of kindness I have experienced over the last few months. Another friend, whom I seldom see, gave me a really good bicycle. Another couple, whom I love dearly, made my car-payment the last two months and friends gave me work and helped in many other ways. The list just goes on and on.

Friends used to say to me quite often, "Sarah, you have such a problem with pride. You love to give, but you have a hard time receiving." I did have a very real problem with pride and I still do. I would rather spring-clean my house than ask for help. Isn't it wonderful how life brings about situations so that we are obligated to work on our own issues. I couldn't turn down offers of help because I wasn't in a position to do so.

So much of life is about giving and receiving, loving and receiving love. Years ago, I paid rent for a co-worker because she and her eleven year old daughter were being evicted and had nowhere to live. Years later, when I was "needy," someone paid my rent. Several years ago, I called the school and offered to help buy a dress for a graduating student whose family could not afford to buy one. This year in spite of being low financially, my daughter has a dress for Homecoming.

As a single mom, don't be afraid or too proud to ask for help. There will probably be a time later when you will be able to help others. Accept love and support from others. They will be blessed as they give. It is a universal law. Giving is returned to us in many ways. Receive and allow others to be blessed. And remember, giving and receiving is not always financial. In fact, what I am writing about has usually nothing to do with money. It is about giving and receiving love and support. Encouraging others and allowing good people into our lives who will do the same for us. We need that, and our children need it also.

Chapter 2

A Time to Heal, A Time to Build Up

When the kids were little I had a vivid dream. A strong gentle hand, holding scissors, cut through the muscle of a large heart, one snip at a time. The hand continued to cut with precision and deliberation. I gazed in awe, knowing that this was my heart. The heart muscle was dark red and healthy but I noted that there was no blood. I looked behind and below the hand of the surgeon. There was no incision. It healed and closed as he cut.

I share this with you because it was a picture of my life. In itself, pain is not bad. In fact, pain is necessary for survival. Our body is full of nerve endings and they are in our body for a good reason. If we stick our hand in the fire those nerve endings alert our brain, in an incredibly short period of time, that our hand needs to be removed from the fire. If we did not remove our hand it would eventually be burned off. Pain is an alert that all is not well.

Emotional pain really is not any different. It is usually a signal to us that we need to change something. Emotional pain is not always a negative experience. We can and do learn so much from our mistakes. We know often, for sure, that we do not want to repeat the same mistake. I believe that many times pain is allowed to happen in our lives for our own growth. Sometimes it appears that a person might die from a broken heart, yet somehow they survive and live to be a stronger person. I'm sure we have all witnessed this and even experienced it in our own lives.

But what about the emotional pain that continues? What about the scars that run deep and cripple us emotionally? So often people are not even aware that those scars are there. We hurt inside and we cover up the pain. Sometimes we deny it and run from it. Everyone else might see the elephant in the middle of the living room but we may appear oblivious to its presence.

The wounds are there however and they need to be healed if we are to lead healthy fulfilling lives. Emotional pain is manifested in many ways, such as irritability, anger, frustration, lack of peace, dissatisfaction, bitterness, resentment, poor self-esteem, self-destructive behavior and, in general, a real lack of happiness.

How can we teach our kids about love if our own lives are full of bitterness, anger and frustration? How can we raise kids with a good, healthy self-esteem when our own is so low? Kids learn by example. The simple truth is, kids do what they see and not what they hear. Treat a child with love and he will be loving. Treat a child with anger and he will be angry. Frustration and criticism of our children will affect their lives, regardless of the amount of love we might feel for them in our hearts.

For many of us, there comes a time when we reach rock-bottom. Everything hurts us emotionally. We are unhappy. There comes a time when we look at other people and see that they are not unhappy. They love themselves and they love their lives. They respect themselves and feel good about who and what they are. Somehow I had lost that or what I had of it before. I wanted to change and grow. I wanted to be happy and free from emotional pain.

I believe that pain will cause us to grow or it will cripple us. Pain presents us with a choice. We embrace it, walk through the pain and emerge a stronger, more loving individual or we harden our hearts and become bitter and angry. I recognized that hardness of heart only robbed me of peace and happiness. By nature, I was a happy person and I did not enjoy unhappiness or depression. I wanted to change. I wanted to grow and be free and happy.

Change is not easy. Embracing our pain and working through it can be very painful. It takes commitment and often we feel like turning back and running into our cocoons or hiding again behind the walls we have created for protection. It means looking at our own accountability and even our weaknesses. It means looking at our own patterns and facing where we may have been responsible. I learned that a lot of emotional pain is caused by unforgiveness and that with forgiveness comes great freedom. I learned that we cannot go through our adult lives blaming others and circumstances.

I learned how to cry and that tears can be cleansing and contribute to our healing. I learned that we will not do well in relationships when we carry with us a lot of baggage that needs to go. And I especially learned that we do not have to stay the same. We can change. It may be tough but it is exciting.

It was fun and exciting to grow with my kids. I hear a lot of people make jokes about Self-help and Positive thinking books. I read so many. I wrote those affirmations and read them daily. I listened to tapes. What I learned, I shared with the kids. Before Suzanne could write and Noah was just learning to write, we wrote goals together.

Healing and growth are necessary in our lives and they are ongoing. Letting go and forgiveness are ongoing. What our children see is usually what they become. Books, tapes, and allowing God's love to come into my life was responsible for a lot of change and healing. If you hurt emotionally, don't be afraid to embrace the pain and work through it. You will like the new loving you and so will your children.

Yes, for everything there is a season under Heaven. A time to heal, A time to build up. We may need to heal, and our kids may need to heal also. And "always" is a time to build up our children. Perhaps together we can heal and be built up. We can grow strong together. My vivid dream is and was a reality. In our lives, our hearts may be cut. Sometimes an incision by the great Surgeon himself and sometimes by our own actions or the actions of others. However, healing follows behind and under the hand the scars are gone, either removed or never formed.

A Tear is a Tear, is it Not?

Many a tear has to fall
But it's all in the game.
All in that wonderful game
That we know as love.

Many a tear does fall, but they are not all in that wonderful game. There are so many different kinds of tears, and I am probably happy about every one that I shed, buckets and buckets of them. If I collected all of them I could probably water my garden for a week or so. Tears are O.K. and we need to remember that.

I hope that you cry sometimes. I don't hope that you are sad all of the time but I hope that you are still able to cry. Able to cry? Yes, because not everyone can cry. It is a blessing to be able to cry, to shed tears. Tears of relief, tears of gladness, tears of joy, tears of healing, tears of letting go, tears of forgiveness, tears of sadness, tears of regret, tears of sorrow, tears because we are glad to be alive, tears that our lives are so much better than they were before, tears that we are getting stronger, tears that our children are so wonderful and we love them so much.

Tears, tears, tears. There were times in my life that I thought I would know nothing but tears. I would see a little girl in the street, and sense that she was not well treated - I would cry. I would see a young girl and sense that she was in a bad marriage - I would cry. I would see couples together and very much in love - I would cry. I would see a lonely old person - I would cry. Sometimes I would cry out, "God, am I going to cry forever?"

I didn't cry forever, but I am glad that I cried buckets of tears for years. It was during all of those tears and all of my pain that I healed day by day. Sometimes my heart hurt so much, I felt that it would break. I feel that it did break. But something very wonderful happened. Someone put it together again. Stronger and healthier than it ever was. Now my heart feels healthy and strong. With time those tears washed away all of that pain and regret.

I still see a little girl and sense that she is not well treated - I may cry silently but it doesn't hurt. I pray for every little girl that hurts. I still see a young girl and sense that she is in a bad marriage - I reach out and be a friend. I see couples together and very much in love - I feel their happiness - I too am loved. Not just by one person but many, many wonderful people. I cried many tears and I am glad. Today, if I were to cry tears, they would be for single parents, especially those who hurt and struggle as I once did. Don't be afraid to cry. Shed those healing, cleansing tears and be strong for your kids. I'm here to tell you that "Tears Work.

Forgive Him? You've Got to be Kidding!

I am not an expert on forgiveness, and I certainly could not write a book about it or expound much on the subject. All I know about forgiveness, is what I have experienced in my own life. Those experiences were so tough at the time, but the reward was great.

Resentment, anger, bitterness. These are heavy words, and most of us do not want to own them in our lives. Does that mean that these things do not exist in our lives? Unfortunately not.

If we did some honest soul searching and dug deep, we might be shocked at the stuff we've shoved deep down in our hearts, so deep that it is covered up. If we were to take the lid off our hearts, as it were a garbage can and start sorting through it. Wow would we get a surprise or two. Resentment, anger and bitterness destroy us. They eat at us and corrode our insides like poison does. They make us sick and cause us so much unnecessary pain and grief. I know because I've been there.

Sometimes there is pain in our hearts and a real lack of peace. I'm only sharing my own experience here but when I hurt, I usually found unforgiveness. I was usually harboring bad feelings. Unforgiveness robbed me of my peace and happiness. With time, I learned that forgiveness brings with it freedom and happiness. I loved the new found freedom. I didn't have to hurt anymore and I didn't have to be angry and in turmoil any more.

Have you ever noticed how anger and frustration just spill all over the place? At work you were blamed for something that you didn't do or didn't mean to do. You arrive home and trip over a toy so you are upset at the kids. Before you know it you are frustrated with the stupid car and tired of that dumb dog that drips water all over the kitchen floor. Ever feel like this? When we feel like this, it is time to stop and look at what we are really upset about. We are not upset at the kids or the car or dog, we are really upset at the boss. Yes, anger has a way of spilling over and affecting every area of our lives.

The kids didn't do anything unusual, the car is the same old car and the dog has dripped water over the kitchen floor for years. If we don't deal with the anger toward our boss, our whole lives are affected. Unresolved anger grows like a cancer and eats at us. All in all, we are pretty miserable individuals.

One night, when my mother was visiting from Ireland, I told her that I was going to call my ex-husband and ask him to forgive me. She said, "Sarah, are you daft?" I will translate for you. In Irish this means, "Sarah, are you crazy?" She thought that I had lost my mind. Maybe I had, but if I did, it was a good thing.

You see, it does take two to tango. I had reacted and contributed to problems. I may not have been the reason for the problems, but none of us are perfect. I was not blameless. I was not a spiritual giant. I was not responsible for how another individual chose to deal with his anger but I was responsible for how I dealt with mine. It didn't matter if the other person was willing to let go. What was important to my own health and well-being, was that I let go and go on with my life. The step that I took that evening brought big changes in my life and, I believe, changes in the life of another individual.

When I asked this person to forgive me, I had no idea of the outcome. All I had was a conviction that this was something I needed to do to in order to go on with my life. The outcome took me by surprise. When I asked that question, it opened a door and I did not hear an angry retort. Instead I heard a question, "Yes, and can you forgive me?" That was the beginning of a wonderful series of lessons on forgiveness.

Until that time, there was a lot of upheaval and friction. It was pretty normal stuff but normal isn't always right. I didn't want to live the rest of my life being angry and resentful and I certainly did not want to live my life in a battle with another individual. We had two children to share for many years to come. I did not want to struggle with this person for the rest of my life and I certainly did not want my children to suffer the consequences of constant friction between their parents.

Anger is not contained and it does overflow into all areas of our lives. You may have every reason to be angry with your ex-spouse. You may be very justified in your anger. However, for your own sake and the sake of your children, I encourage you to let go of that resentment. It will keep you from growing and moving forward. It will affect your relationships to come and it will steal the peace that you deserve as you raise your children.

It just is not worth the grief and turmoil. Forgiveness and letting go is a process that we go through all of our lives, day after day. Many times we will be required to forgive and many times it will be necessary to let go.

That night on the phone did not end the occasional conflicts that I had with my children's father. Parents have conflicts whether they are married or divorced and they need to be worked out. It isn't easy but don't waste your life being angry about someone or something over which you have no control.

Remember that forgiveness is not an emotion, it is an action, something we do. It is a choice. We do not always feel forgiveness but we make a choice to forgive. As we determine to do it, we may not feel it, but we choose to do it anyway. With time it becomes a reality. We may feel the anger and frustration, but we continue to choose to let go and move forward. Believe me, it is worth every ounce of energy invested.

Regardless of how or why divorce happens, it is not an easy transition. Divorce carries with it many things. Disappointment, disillusionment, pain, regret, abandonment, rejection, loneliness, fear, devastation and hopelessness are but a few of the feelings that we might experience. Even if we are relieved to be out of the relationship, we may experience some or all of these.

Divorce is harsh, even if it was necessary for our survival. Once I heard an illustration of divorce and marriage. It was explained like this. Marriage is like two young trees planted very close together. With time, the young trees intertwine and wrap around each other, becoming like one tree, strong and solid. It's a great picture of marriage and serves to illustrate why divorce is so devastating.

In the picture of divorce, this tree is severed down the middle so that the two trees can grow separately. The severing cuts through each tree as it slices from top to bottom. The roots are intertwined also. The tree bleeds and is weakened close to death.

I do not tell you this illustration to make you feel guilty or go running back to your spouse, I used this illustration to bring to all of our minds the trauma of divorce. The need for our divorce may have been a matter of life and death and we may know great relief but deep down there is usually trauma, even if it is just the fact that we are now faced with raising children alone.

This may not apply to all but some of you at one time had strong feelings about the father of your children. There was once a time when all you wanted was to be with this person. Being around him made you feel like the happiest woman in the world. You had dreams together and built a home together. Best of all, you had wonderful kids together.

Why do I bring this up and remind you? Because, regardless of the reason for your divorce, it stands to reason that there is disappointment and possibly disillusionment in your life. It is very normal to be disappointed and even angry under these circumstances. Don't be ashamed of your disappointment and don't deny those feelings. Work with the anger and face up to the disappointment. They are valid feelings. You had hopes and dreams and they have been shattered.

When I first left I was relieved to be out of the relationship and start a new life. It was a good and necessary move. I was in survival mode and had to support and raise two tiny children. I didn't have time for introspection or self analysis. I had turned the page and walked into the next chapter of my life.

It was a rough chapter and I had a lot of necessary healing to go through, not to mention growing up. I strove to forgive the "him" that we all need to forgive and asked that he forgive me. I had regrets about the mess that I had made of my life but it didn't occur to me for many years how disappointed I was that my marriage had failed. I know that without a miracle, the marriage would never have worked. Only several years ago did it hit me that we would never be a complete family.

Divorce is a harsh blow whether welcomed or not. Many realities surround it. Regardless, we need to forgive and move on.

Dad

My Dad passed away last spring, very suddenly after experienced a massive stroke from which he never regained consciousness. Several years earlier, he had experienced his first stroke.

I must admit he was a real trooper. Some people give up after a stroke. My Dad went on with his life as if it had never happened. His speech was ever so slightly impaired and his limp was notable only when he was tired. He made his second trip to California after his stroke and we made a trip to Disneyland. He made the rounds at Disneyland and never complained.

Yes, he was a trooper. But like every parent, myself included, he was far from perfect. Parents do what their own parents did. So, I must admit, I did have a few hang-ups. But, we can't hang on to the past. We need to release and move on.

Forgiveness is not easy. In fact, it is so difficult! When we forgive it means that the other person goes free. It does not mean that the other person did not not do something to hurt us, but we accept the pain and the person is free of charges. Forgiveness is not a word to use lightly. Forgiveness is a deeply spiritual act. Some of you have been called upon to forgive a lot will know what I am attempting to say.

The awesome thing about forgiveness is that it is not just for the other person (the forgiven), it is even more wonderful for the forgiver. Because until we forgive, we are prisoners. We are emotionally crippled. We clutch the pain and the hurt. When we forgive, we are released. Better still, when we forgive, we are forgiven. Next chance you have, read "The Lord's Prayer". *"Forgive me, as I have forgiven others"*.

Up until several years ago, I knew little about my Dad's childhood. What kind of childhood did he have? What kind of male role model did he have in his life? He did not live with his father. Shortly after World War One, when he was a baby, my dad's father left for New York like so many young men in Ireland were doing at the time. The plan was for all three of them to be reunited in New York when things were settled. Baby Billy and his Mom never did make it to New York. When you think about it, traveling to New York via boat in 1923 with a two year old is certainly different than hopping on a jet in 1995. So, my Dad and his Mom were alone. His Dad did send money on a regular basis.

Sometimes I find myself asking, "Doesn't it come naturally to us, how to raise kids?". My own conclusion is that to some of us it is a natural thing. Perhaps it is the loving part that comes naturally. The how part is where we tend to get lost.

Today we have books galore on how to raise kids. It is on television and on the radio. It seems like it is everywhere. We have not turns into super parents with perfect kids as a result of reading these books. However, the public on the whole is more aware of the effects that environment has on children and their self-esteem.

We know for instance that if we beat and abuse our children, we are communicating to them violence is a way of life and is okay. Children need love and discipline to reach their full potential as individuals, not abuse and violence.

We know that a child who witnesses his father hitting his mother, even though he despises this treatment of the mother he loves, will likely mistreat his own wife one day. We know without a doubt that a child who is ridiculed or publically shamed by his parents will recoil and may become shy, awkward or insecure. Even teasing by a well-meaning parent can be harmful. Some children are not affected by teasing, while a child in the same family may be traumatized by that teasing.

Parents, do not ridicule your children or shame them. Do not make fun of their bodies, or any little imperfections they might have. Life is tough enough for children and teenagers. Build them up, discipline when you must, but never tear your children down in any way. Most parents know not to be insensitive but some do not. They are simply repeating the pattern.

Be kind and gracious with your parents. This is a repeat but I do venture to guess that most parents are doing the best they can with the knowledge they have. Unfortunately babies do not come with instructions. Children are not raised by robots. They are raised by people who have needs and are not perfect.

My parents were born post World War One and lived through a second World War, the center of which was just across a short stretch of water. Ireland was already a poor country but the economy of Britain was atrocious after two world wars. Our parents knew poverty and saw some loved ones die. Just this morning, I hung a picture of my grandfather (my mother's father) and his six brothers, all dressed in uniform to go off to World War One. Life was rough back then.

When patterns repeat in our lives, we need to take a good look at what is going on and question why we do the things we do. The good news is that we can all change. We don't have to stay the way we are. Yippee. I am glad that I'm not the same person I was ten years ago (I'm sure other people are happy about that also), and that I'm not the same person I will be ten years from now.

Don't Blame Your Parents

A couple of years ago, I was talking to my son. He was relating to me a conversation he had shared with a friend who was also being raised by a single parent. She had commented to him, "At least your parents are friends and get along." His response was, "You know, there comes a time when we can't blame our parents for our circumstances. We have to be responsible for our own lives." Wise words for a sixteen year old.

Wish I had known that when I was sixteen, but I do now and that's what matters. No more a victim but a person with accountability.

There are few of us who do not have regrets about how we were raised. Some of us have deep emotional and possibly physical scars from abusive treatment. Some of us were raised with little money and have sad memories of how it was to go without. And even some of us were raised with lots of money, which was supposed to replace the love, approval and quality time that we desperately needed from our parents.

I watched the movie "Stand by Me." It was an exceptionally well written script, adapted from Stephen King's, "The Body." The movie is about four adolescent boys who set out on a search to find a dead body. It is a great movie and made a great impression on me. Perhaps, because I have learned that regardless of ethnic, cultural or economic background, each of us has a "little cross to bear."

The movie floored me! Four boys with, different backgrounds and different parenting styles. One boy came from a "bad" family, with a "bad" reputation. He was destined to fail. The next boy had been quite severely abused and was emotionally unstable. His father was in "an insane asylum." The third boy was somewhat obese, over protected by an over-indulgent mother and was afraid of his own shadow. The fourth boy, the narrator of the story, was a gifted writer.

His teenage brother, an up and coming athlete, had recently died. His parents were so consumed with their own grief that they failed to see the boy's grief and his wonderful gift of writing.

At the end of the movie, the outcome of each of the boy's lives is shared. The boy from the "bad" family, in spite of his pain and disadvantages, went on to become an attorney. I am only presuming here, that because of the injustice that he had experienced in his own life, he had compassion for those who were unfairly treated. He tried to defend such a victim one night in a restaurant and died from a fatal stab wound. The over indulged child, I believe did not venture from his home-town. The abused child went on to live his unhappy life. The child who was neglected due to his parents' engulfing grief went on to become a famous writer.

The story is fictional, but I share it to make a point. To a large degree, we have control of our lives. Some of us hurt profoundly from our childhood and God forbid that anyone would ever make light of that fact. My heart hurts to hear the gruesome stories. This I do know. We can all change. Sometimes, as I walk through life, I rub shoulders with exceptional individuals. It always takes me by surprise when one such individual shares what disadvantages he/she experienced in childhood. Why do some move on and do great things with their lives, while others remain defeated and hurting?

I believe that it is because these great individuals have learned an invaluable truth: that as adults, we alone are responsible for our own lives. We are accountable. We cannot blame our parents forever. We, as individuals have incredible potential to overcome. Insurmountable as it might appear to some, we can change, we can overcome. Sometimes we need a dose of Tough Love. In a nutshell, if you don't like it, change it.

Some of you might be saying already (and I would be foolish to dispute the point), "Oh, but your parents weren't like mine." I'm not making light of anyone's grief here. I just know that we cannot afford to go on blaming our parents or anything else.

Yes, we are victims and yes, some of us hurt. However, until we let go, we will never heal. Now that we are adults, we are responsible for our own lives and what we make of them. The choice is ours. Yes, we might be justified in hating a parent but that will not make our lives better or easier.

Becoming responsible and accountable is what makes our lives better. Yes, we were victims but now, as adults, we can choose not to be victims and learn not to victimize. Change is not easy. It is a lot of work and it takes time. But I am here to share with you that change is exciting and rewarding. And after all, isn't life a journey? It is not just about having or gaining material things, although that in itself is not wrong. On a journey, we move from A to B. En route, there are many changes. Changes of scenery, changes of seasons. Enjoy the seasons and don't forget to smell the roses.

Learn what you can from every experience. A crisis is an opportunity for growth. Be thankful for the bad experiences as well as the good ones. Embrace those hard times and know that this would not happen to you if you were not capable of overcoming. Remember, the snow has to fall and remain on the ground before that beautiful and delicate little Snow-drop appears. Be thankful. Embrace that cold harsh snow and be a beautiful Snow-drop.

On Behalf of Parents

It is difficult to write this because I realize that many had huge crosses to bear during their childhood, but I need to write it anyway.

You see, I believe with all my heart that most parents do not fail their children because they are "bad" people. Most of our parents were doing their best, the very best they could with the knowledge and understanding they had. Some had fathers who were so busy providing for the family, that they were seldom home. Those fathers probably did not have a clue that you had emotional needs that were not being met. They thought that as long as they were meeting your physical needs, they were being good fathers, and they were. Some of you might say, "my father never told me that he loved me." He probably did not know that he needed to tell you that he loved you. He probably assumed that you knew this. After all, didn't he work hard to provide for your needs?

Also important is the fact that our parents modeled their own parents. If their parents did not demonstrate love and affection, they probably did not even think of being loving and affectionate toward us. Now love and affection are wonderful, and I wish that every one of us had experienced both but the lack of both does not mean that our parents did not love us. They just did not know. They were not raised to be loving and affectionate.

Some of us had parents who were angry and verbal. We were shattered and demeaned, yet this outburst did not even phase the parent. This parent probably had a parent(s) who was angry and verbal. I am not justifying this parent's behavior, but I do believe that this behavior was probably learned from his parent.

I venture to say that the majority of our parents raised us the way they were raised and feel that they did a good job. After all, we turned out O.K., didn't we? A lot of us know that we didn't. Some of us traveled a rough road on the inside, even though we looked O.K. on the outside.

Now as adults we understand more. Most of us are able to say, "My parents love me. I can't stand their parenting style, but they did love me." Don't criticize your parents. Strive in your heart to know that they did their best. Remember, they had their trials and hard times. I know that for some, this is difficult - just try any way.

When is the last time you called your parents and told them that you loved them? Reach out to them. Remember, if you are hurting, they may be hurting even more. Call them and say, "Thank you for raising me." Better still, say, "Thank you for loving me." Then stand back and watch the, healing begin.

The Pain of Regret

Sometimes I meet folks and we get to sharing. I can scarcely believe the number of them who say to me things like, "I don't know where my son is" or, "My daughter hasn't spoken to me for years" or, "My parents disowned me". I can't even start to fathom this pain.

Find your son, write a letter to your daughter, go to your parents. Make amends before it is too late. The pain of regret is a heavy. Especially if the person has left this earth and we cry out daily, "Please tell my dad that I am so sorry", and we never know if he knows how sorry we are.

The pain of regret can be true grief. If there is any way of avoiding that pain, do it now. Pick up the phone, write that letter, take a trip if needs be. Do it now. Find that someone. Be willing to make the first move. You won't regret it!

Forgiveness is not a word to use lightly. Forgiveness is a deeply spiritual act. Some of you who have been called on to forgive a lot will know what I am attempting to say. The awesome thing about forgiveness is that it is not just for the other person (the forgiven), it is even more wonderful for the forgiver. Because, until we forgive, we are prisoners. We are emotionally crippled. We clutch the pain and hurt. When we forgive, we are released.

Better still, when we forgive, we are forgiven. Next chance you have, read "The Lord's Prayer". "Forgive me, as I have forgiven others."

The Serenity Prayer

Lord, Grant me the serenity to
Accept the things I cannot change.
Courage to change the things I can,
And the wisdom to know the difference.

This prayer has come to mean a lot to me, and I wish I could remember it many times a day. How different my life would be, from day to day, if I had it before me always. It says so much and I don't think I need to explain. There are some things that we cannot change. There are things we can change but change takes courage, boldness and often means a lot of work on our parts. The most wonderful part is the wisdom to know the difference between the things we can change and the things over which we have no control. There is a world of difference. That difference can mean serenity or turmoil.

The first time I heard this prayer was at an Al Anon meeting. Al Anon is a group for those affected in some way by someone else's drinking. I do not even remember how I first heard about this group but I remember the warmth and love that I experienced at that meeting. I was surrounded by people who cared and understood what I was feeling. You see, I did not even understand myself, the awful confusion and pain that had become so much part of my life.

On my knee sat the person closest to me in the whole world. He was about eighteen months old, had blonde curly ringlets, and eyes as deep as the ocean. He was a happy baby and had no clue as to the unhappy world in which his mother lived, day after day.

That meeting was possibly the turning point in my life. Before the meeting, I died a million deaths a day. Those of you who have had this experience will relate to what I am saying. You will remember the pain and anguish of living in the deceptive world of alcoholism. The great need to escape but the paralysis and denial that suffocates us day after day. Not to mention the grief we experience as we watch the person we married become the stranger we no longer know and understand.

Going to the meeting took a lot, of guts, but I had reached rock bottom. I feared that I was betraying another individual. This person needed my help, not my betrayal. My fears were relieved. Nothing shared in that room would ever be shared outside of that room. What a great comfort it was to know that I was surrounded by people who would never share that secret. I was more than surprised at those whom I saw at the meeting, but that surprise was never shared with another person.

Before I went to the meeting, I had actually reached the point where I felt that I might be insane. Sometimes I would pinch myself to see if I was real. Day after day I was told that I concocted accounts of events. They did not really happen. What do you mean they did not happen? I was right here. I heard and I saw. Yes, I was conscious and did hear and see. That person was there also and heard and saw. My mind was in turmoil day after day. How could someone not remember the awful scenes from the evening before?

I knew nothing about the disease of alcoholism. The buried pain, denial and deception. I did not know that someone could experience things and deny their occurrence, or simply not remember. I did not know that a sane and very intelligent person could get out of bed the next morning and simply not recall or admit the terrible scenes from the night before.

I picked up the courage to speak and the folks in the room listened with love and patience. They reached out to me and shared their own experiences. I wasn't crazy. I cried and cried. I was not crazy after all. Hallelujah (I didn't know about hallelujahs back then). Those meetings were wonderful. I did not have to fill in the details from the night before. I was not responsible and it would have been denied anyway.

Better still, I learned that I had no control over someone else's drinking. "Another individual's drinking did not depend on how good or how bad a person I was. I did not have to strive to be a super human being in the hope that another person would not drink. I did not have to tip-toe around and live in fear of upsetting someone because conflict might make them drink more. In other words, I had no control, or I did not have to control. All the control in the world would not put an end to the cycle. I learned also, not to hide and cover up.

Yes, I cared and I hurt as I watched our worlds crumble, but I could not change it. I could not control another person's path in life. Have you ever tried to love with detachment? It sounds a lot easier than it is to actually do. It is a lot easier to write about now than it was to do at the time and, actually, I probably did a lousy job.

In fact, I blew it constantly. Many, many times I did the very things I was taught not to do. I nagged, I tried to control, I argued back, I retaliated. Many times I did all of the "No No's." Many times though, I remembered and practiced the things I learned in Al Anon and made major breakthroughs. I lived one day at a time. I was the opposite of a spiritual giant, but I know that I tried, one day at a time.

Then of course, there is the anger and the frustration. Anger, because you know that one day you will have to leave and the other person is not cooperating and making an effort to help change the situation. Hopelessness, because there is nothing you can do to make the situation any better. Fear, because you know that you will be alone raising children, and what does the future hold? Sadness, because the love and-respect is gone, and- in it-'s place is pity, defeat and disillusionment.

While all of this is going on, you take care of business and try to hold life together for all involved. You struggle to stay sane and survive the crisis, one day at a time. Then the day comes when you know in your heart, that for the sake of your own sanity, you must leave the comfort zone. As uncomfortable as it might be, at least it is the life we know and it is predictable. You know what will be happening tomorrow.

Anyway, by this time, all of your confidence has been chiseled away. You feel unloved and unlovable. You no longer believe in yourself, or your ability to start a new life, move to a new area and raise kids alone. It is an awesome thought.

Those years at Happy Acre, I forgot the serenity prayer and I no longer went to Al Anon. I moved out into the woods and started a new life, far from the maddening crowd. It was a time of healing, and that healing took a long time. Now, I read and pray the Serenity Prayer often. There were things I could not change. I was a single mother. With time I accepted that. As time passed, I accepted that there was no knight in shining armor to rescue me and make life easier. What a blessing it was to accept this with serenity; and serenity is what I felt when I learned to be happy with myself. No individual could wave a magic wand and make me happy. Happiness lay in my own heart, and only myself held the key to happiness.

I could not change the fact that my children only had one parent. It hurt that I could not be a mother and a father to them, and I could not wave a magic wand and produce a father. Again, I found serenity as I endeavored to be a special mother to them?

Change does take courage, and change can hurt. Not necessarily the changing itself, but looking honestly at ourselves and seeing the areas that need to change can be ruthless. Sometimes friends tell us things about ourselves, and we do not want to accept what they tell us. Usually, we are angry and deny what is told to us. Our flaws are difficult to accept. It often means that we have to look inside ourselves and admit that there is a problem. But if we do not look to see if there is any truth in what is being told to us, how will we ever grow and change? There were times, at Happy Acre, that people told me things about myself. It hurt. I was already so vulnerable, how could I face dealing with more flaws. My self-esteem was already so low that I could hardly face looking at those problems. But, I made a commitment to at least look. Sometimes I cried and felt that I would die, but I determined to change and be different.

Sometimes people say things to hurt us when they are angry, and I'm learning to consider the source. That is not what I am talking about. I'm talking about the advice that people who love us share with us. I'm talking about repeated patterns in our lives that cause problems. Often, we need to look within ourselves. There just might be a problem there.

I've had to look at many patterns in my life, and you know what? The problem was not fate and the problem was not other people, the problem was all mine.

It takes courage to change the things we can, and it takes a lot of courage to change ourselves. It is not our job in life to change or control others. The only person we can change is ourselves. Most of the time, we want to change the people around us and the circumstances in our lives. This is not about courage. This is control.

I wish I could remember to apply this prayer to all the situations in my life. The serenity to accept the things I cannot change. The courage to change the things I can, especially me and leave everyone else alone, AND, the wisdom to know the difference. WISDOM. A small word with a big meaning.

A lot has happened since that first Al Anon meeting, when I felt as if I had walked into the most wonderful place on earth and hot tears rolled down my face as those in that little room reached out in love. I couldn't see the forest for the trees. I was so busy learning that there were things in life over which I had no control, I never got to the next line. Now I love all of it. Now, most of the time, if I stop and think long enough, I find that there is wisdom to know the difference.

Now, I endeavor to let go and pray. I have no control, but I know someone who does. Thank you, Jesus.

From Rags to Riches

A classic picture is conjured up in our minds when we think of "Rags to Riches." Personally, I love to hear success stories and true Cinderella stories. But that is not what I am talking about here.

I am talking about being rich in soul and spirit. The opposite of which is being impoverished in soul and spirit. Have you been there? I have and I do not want to be there ever again. Not ever. It is a sad place to be. Maybe some of you know exactly what I mean. I can truly say, "Once I was in rags, now I am rich."

Once my life was so tough. Not just because I was a single mom, struggling to raise two kids alone, but because I had so much pain and garbage in my life. My self esteem was rock bottom, my self image was disastrous and I had little hope. I guess I had sunk as low as a person could sink. I felt unloved and unlovable. I had no confidence and did not believe in myself.

Events had happened in my life to bring about this decline. I say decline because I had not always felt like this. I left Ireland when I was twenty-one, full of dreams and anticipating many wonderful adventures. So many dreams had come true for me. I went to Canada and had a wonderful time. A friend and myself packed our backpacks and went off to Europe for a year. It was pretty incredible. We lived in places in Europe for months at a time.

We traveled across North Africa and I could write a book about the experiences we had there. I lived in Greece for four months and visited the Greek Islands by working on boats there. Later I went back to Canada where I went to university and majored in Fine Art, which was the fulfillment of yet another dream.

My life did change though and all my confidence was gone. Actually, I was pretty shattered. It was tough on my mom because she knew how I used to be. She wondered where the old Sarah had gone.

It took many years to grow and change. My life was filled with people who loved me and believed in me, even when I did not believe in myself. I was afraid of my own shadow and I was so negative and pathetic. I wasn't much fun to be around.

Today my life is so different, and I praise the Lord for that and thank all of those wonderful people who loved me in spite of myself. Today, my life is so rich and so blessed. Do I have hope? Lots of it! Do I like myself? Yes, I do! Do I love my life? Very much so. Better still, I have peace that I didn't know was possible, even if life isn't going as I plan it.

I have two wonderful kids. I do not have a lot of money because I do crazy things like going to Ireland and taking time off so that I can write this book and hopefully encourage you, who are raising children alone. I am broke, but that is a temporary state. I live in an adorable little house in a beautiful town where I know lots of people.

Right now my life is going through so many changes, but it is not stressful. It is not stressful because I believe that whatever direction my life is led, it will be good. The Lord is in control. These last few months have been the happiest in my life. My life truly is so blessed. Those early years were so tough, but they have passed. Now I am in my forties and my life has done a complete turn around.

I worked hard and strove to grow, no matter what the cost. Now so many doors have opened up to me and I have time to do things that I had to put on the back burner for so long. My life is full of people who care and encourage me to move forward.

My biggest dream of all was to write about being a single mom so that y'all would know that you are not alone in your trials. Today, I am writing that book. It may never be published, but it has given me much pleasure to write it.

If you are discouraged and feel like your life is on the rocks, look up. There is hope. Remember, you are a beautiful, wonderful person, "cuz God don't make no junk." Someone or something along the way may have told you that you are a failure and unlovable - it isn't true.

You are special. Don't let anyone tell you differently and don't let anyone steal your dream. Be all that you can be and move from "rags to riches."

Une Petite Revelation

I do not know why I reverted to French to describe this revelation. But the following truly was a realization, or small revelation, to me. To others ths may have been common knowledge, but at thirty years old I had not quite figure this out. There was so much that I did not know.

It was an absolutely beautiful spring morning. The sky was blue and the air was crisp. The weather was starting to warm up, but not enough to not need a fire and firewood to burn in the stove. We had been on our own for about five months now, and we had a routine. We were adapting to country living in the woods. We struggled financially, but we were happy with our new lives. In fact, we were very blessed beyond words.

I was still underweight and scrawny but the sea air, sunshine and exercise of country living made me feel strong and alive. We were splitting wood for our big wood stove that we had grown to enjoy so much. Suzanne delighted herself in the two new puppies. What a little treat she was. She was so tiny; sometimes I wondered how those little legs could run around so many hours a day on that happy acre with all the adventures it held for these happy, inquisitive children. Her hair, very blonde and wispy, only served to accentuate her white skin and deep blue eyes. Her hair refused to grow. Today, her hair is so thick and abundant that she often threatens to have it thinned. That day as she chased after the puppies, I would not have believed that she would end up with such a beautiful head of hair.

Noah, who was only three years old at this time, already had strong personality traits. He had a happy, sunny disposition and loved life to the max. Already, he could read quite well and loved books and stories. He and I were pioneers. It was our job to split the wood and light the fire.

We were a great team. I split the wood and as the logs fell to the side, Noah loaded them into the wheel-barrow. He worked hard and took great pride in his work. We enjoyed working together. When the wheel-barrow was full, together we would wheel it to the carport. He unloaded the wheel-barrow, brought it back to the wood pile and proceeded to fill it again.

Inside, my mother was cooking up something very delicious, and we knew that a wonderful treat was in store. I do not know what I was even thinking about as Noah and I continued to store split wood except that I was happy and content. Maybe that is how revelations come to us. I certainly was not thinking about a relationship and the last thing on my mind was meeting Sir Galahad. That was the last thing on my mind back in those days.

I really do not know where this came from, but suddenly I was thinking, "fifty percent and fifty percent does not make one hundred percent in a relationship, it makes fifty percent. One hundred percent and one hundred percent in a relationship does not make two hundred percent. It makes one hundred percent." This was exciting stuff.

Often the thinking is, if I could just meet that other person who understands me and treats me well, my contribution and his contribution would amount to a good relationship. My fifty percent and his fifty percent would add up to one hundred percent. I realized, with sirens going off, that this was erroneous thinking. If I was not a complete person, no relationship would ever make me a complete person. Being complete and fulfilled was something that had to happen within me. I had to be a whole person who felt good about who I was and what I was doing. This had to happen for me and was not the responsibility of the man that I might someday choose to spend my life with.

With this realization, I understood also that I could not make up the other fifty percent for a man. If he was only fifty percent and looking for a friend who would add up to the other fifty percent, I would never meet that need. He had to find the answer within himself. I knew that I would not ever meet that need. I wanted to be with a man who was happy with himself and not waiting for a special someone to make his life right.

I'm not saying that two people cannot love each other through trials and grow together, that is a big part of what marriage is all about. I did realize though that myself a wounded person and another wounded person did not automatically go together. Before I could ever consider being in a relationship, I needed to heal, grow and feel complete and secure about who I was.

I was elated. I had been in a relationship where neither, the other person or myself were prepared for a marriage relationship. I was now challenged to experience contentment and fulfillment as a single person before I ever considered marriage. At this point what did I have to offer other than my own pain and regret. In the meantime, I would be content to heal, raise my children and become a whole person, better than ever before.

I split a lot of wood after that day, and each time I was out there splitting wood, I thought about how wonderful it was to have another chance in life and how good it was to be single, alone with my two children and growing with them, day by day.

There were times when it would have been great to have someone to share my life with, but deep down I knew that the time was not right. If I ever married again, it would be very special. Something that special is worth waiting for. I needed to be patient and concentrate on the tasks at hand. For today, that was raising my children and growing to become a complete and healthy person.

Over the Years

A lot has happened over the years since the kids were so young. Just recently I came across an affirmation which I had written. "I am bold and confident in dealing with people." I affirmed it and I reaffirmed it daily. In those days, I was neither bold nor confident. I allowed situations to exist in our lives because I could not say, "No" or stand up for myself. I still tend to avoid confrontation, and I do not handle friction well. But I am aware of this, and I continue to work on it. However, I am bold when I need to be, and I am confident in dealing with people. It did not happen overnight. It was a long, slow process.

Today, friends only laugh when I tell them how I used to be. Seventeen years ago, I could not have taught a class to a group of nurses or functioned as a Director of Nurses. Over the last seven years, all of these things were quite natural for me. Back in those days, negative things happened and I was overwhelmed. Today negative things still occur in my life. Yes, sometimes I may be temporarily overwhelmed and discouraged, but today I have a whole new belief system. I believe that everything in our lives happens for a reason and that, always, good will come out of a situation. Today I say, "What am I meant to learn from this?" Crisis is an opportunity for growth.

Today I look to see where I am accountable and check my motives. I do not always like what I see, but I am responsible.

As for unforgiveness? Well I believe now, more than ever, that unforgiveness is capable of making us physically and emotionally ill. It cripples us and robs us of our health and happiness. I don't mean to make light of this, and I have not been required to forgive a person for taking the life of someone I love. I do know though, that the consequences of unforgiveness are tough. Forgiveness is ongoing in our lives and we are forever, it seems, "Letting Go."

Over the years I have had some very unfair and unjust experiences. Yes, I could have retaliated. I could have fought and won. Usually though, I dusted off my feet. You see, the laws of sowing and reaping are forever at work. No one escapes these laws. I do not have to waste time and energy, or even my health on revenge or unforgiveness. I'm not saying that I never struggle with anger or bad feelings when someone wrongs me. I am far from perfect. But, I do not need to seek revenge.

It all never ceases to amaze me. Sometimes, letting go is such a struggle, and sometimes it takes a while. I could share many stories of how I witnessed the laws of sewing and reaping at work. More than once, I have lost well paid jobs because someone in power actually lied about me and built a case against me. Sometimes letting go did come slowly, but I moved forward in my life only to witness, sometime down the road, the same turn of events take place in the life of the one who had wronged me. I didn't sit around and gloat, waiting for this to happen. That is not what letting go is all about. But the law of sewing and reaping is a reality that every person deals with.

Knowing this helps me to remember my own actions, because I see those laws at work in my own life. I just remembered something that happened long ago in Ireland. I was about eighteen and a new nursing student. Seeing someone die, holding their hand as they did so was a brand new experience for me. He was reassuring, me, when it was supposed to be the other way around. He held my hand. He said, "Dear, I've lived a good life and I am ready to leave this earth." I listened to him as he spoke softly about his life. His face was sweet and there was no fear or anguish. I asked him what he had learned most in his life. He said, "Always do unto others as you would have them do unto you." Then he died.

At ninety-three, he knew the universal law. "Whatsoever a man soweth; that shall he also reap". I wish that I could remember this daily in my own life. And I hope that I have taught this to my kids.

As for mistakes; I still make them, and I will make them probably until I leave this earth. But that is O.K. Because now, I believe that there is no such thing as failure, and that every incident that may look like a mistake or failure only brings us closer to success, closer to the answer or what we should be doing. Mistakes serve as feedback. How can we grow if we never make a mistake?

Babies are a great example to us. Everything is new and exciting to them. They are undaunted. They fall down and they get back up. They make mistakes, but they keep going and soon they can walk and talk. They are the "Bee's knees" as we would say in Ireland. So often though, as adults, we are afraid to make mistakes, afraid to try new things because we might fail or we might screw up. But if we don't push a door, it will never open. We need to keep pushing doors until we find the correct one.

We learn from our mistakes. Thomas Edison made so many "mistakes" before he produced his light bulb. As for Failures? Abe Lincoln struggled for decades before he became President at sixty. He became a great Leader in our country. What if he had given up because he had a few failures?

I've tried so many ventures in my life so far in search of the right livelihood. To others, these ventures may look like failures. To me, earlier they felt like failures. Now I consider them adventures, and I wouldn't change any of them. I've done a lot in my life so far, and I plan to do so much more. The kids survived the adventures, and I hope that they learned from them. I hope that they will be adventurous and willing to go out and try new things and not be afraid of failure.

I'm glad I cried buckets of tears, and I hope that I never loose the compassion I feel for those who hurt. Life is still difficult at times, but I am stronger now. I know that it is not what happens to us in life that matters, but how we as individuals deal with what is happening. I know now that every problem has a solution, and this is what I have tried to pass on to my children. Find the solution.

And, I still try to remember the Serenity prayer:

> Lord, grant me the serenity to
> accept the things I cannot change,
> Courage to change the things I can,
> and the wisdom to know the difference.

Chapter 3

A Time to Break Down, A Time to Build Up

Sure there were bad times, but what I remember most are those sweet times. Those every day little special things, like just being together. I actually miss them now more than ever, because my kids are at the age where it appears that they don't need me. Now I know that is not true, that they do need me, but I sure miss the closeness and togetherness we had when they were younger.

When our kids are little, they need us so much, and they need so much attention. Take my advice and enjoy it to the max. Enjoy them while they are little, because time goes by so fast and in no time it seems like they move away from us. Actually, they do move away. It is a natural part of growth.

If your kids are little, you probably feel like that day when they will not need you is very far away. Believe me, it is just around the corner. Make the most of every day. Create wonderful, loving memories for them and with them. Memories that they can hold on to. Let them know how special they are and what wonderful little individuals they are.

If you are a single parent, it is highly probable that you experienced a divorce. Your children experienced the same divorce. That divorce may be very much to their advantage, but it may still have been somewhat traumatic. With all the strength you can muster up, love them twice as much. And I do not mean, spoil them. Spend time with them. Sit down and be at eye level with them and listen to what they have to say. Let them know that what they have to say is important, and that their feelings are valid, no matter how silly they might seem. This is how we develop good self esteem in our children. You are probably exhausted at the end of the day and still have hours of work ahead of you, but do your utmost to set apart a time that is just for them.

When my kids were little, I was fortunate to listen to a tape by a well known speaker who shared that the most receptive time in a child's day is just before he goes to sleep. What a gold mine of a discovery that was for me, because that was when I had the most time to spend with the kids. We had a set bedtime. Kids like routine and I think that the routine and consistency makes them feel more secure. Bedtime was "Happy Hour" at our house (It was probably a lot more than an hour). "Happy Hour at Happy Acre." That time was theirs. We read a lot, we prayed together and we talked. There were a few nights when I asked Noah to read because I was so tired.

We sure had some fun nights. I remember one night we were reading "Bambi." The pictures in the book were beautiful. There was a picture of Thumper lying on the ground on his back. He was holding his tummy and laughing so hard that tears were coming out of his eyes. Thumper was laughing at Bambi who was learning to talk and called Skunk a flower. Thumper knew that Skunk did not smell like a flower and he just thought that it was all so hilarious. Suzanne, who was around two years old and a little animal lover, was so upset because Thumper was crying. After all, he was lying on the ground and those big tears were coming out of his eyes. So she cried and cried. She loved Thumper and someone had done something very, very bad to him. It was quite the dilemma in our happy little home. Noah and I tried to convince her that Thumper was laughing. I lay down on the floor (the things we do for our kids) on my back, just like Thumper and pretended to laugh. How do you do a Thumper, laughing till you cry act?? Suzanne finally stopped crying and just stared at me like I had lost my marbles. What is that foolish mother of mine doing, lying on the floor? Noah was jumping up and down, laughing and saying, "See Suzanne, Thumper is laughing." The light went on and we saw those little pearly white teeth. "Thumper laughing" That is when the whole thing struck us as being hilarious. Suzanne had a very wet face from crying, yet she was giggling and repeating "Thumper laughing." Noah was exhausted from the excitement and jumping up and down, trying to help his little sis, and this crazy woman was lying on her back in the middle of the bedroom floor, arms and legs in the air like a stuck sheep. That's when we all got to laughing like Thumper, holding our tummies, rolling on the floor with tears coming out of our eyes.

Another night I was so tired that I believe I was "Rummy." The kids were tucked in and I was getting around to my final good night. I started rambling about my crazy day at work. I scurried from bed to bed as I related my story, running from patient to patient. Mrs. So and So was climbing over the side rail and I ran to save her. Mr. So and So yanked his I.V. out and I ran as if to stop him. And Mr. So and So was out in the corridor with no clothes on, so I pretended to chase someone who wasn't there. This little pantomime was not planned and wasn't really meant to be funny, but it sure struck the kids that way. They howled - yet more hysteria. For weeks I listened to requests for "Mom, do your work."

By now you might be saying to yourself, "I am so tired in the evenings and I have so much still to do." Sometimes I used to cry from plain old tiredness. Actually tiredness is an understatement. I was so exhausted that my body hurt, my brain hurt, and sometimes it seemed that my heart even hurt from tiredness. I know that there are times when you feel that you can't keep going. But you will and you do because your children need you too. Take time out of your busy day, even if it is only ten minutes lying on the bed with them, all of you bonding and being close. You can all be tired together.

Worst part about lying down with them is that you have to get up again, and get started. After I tucked the kids in to bed, I would then do the dishes, fold laundry, tidy the house (I can't stand to come home to a messy house) and prepare for the morning exodus!! Aren't the mornings the worst?

All I am saying, single moms/dads, is that the sacrifice is well worth it in the long run. It is straight from my heart. I don't believe that anything can replace close times with our kids. It is the meat that feeds and inspires us single parents. Actually those close times are important for all kids and parents, but I feel that kids from single parent families need a little extra dose of love, and that single moms/dads need an extra dose of encouragement.

You might also be saying to yourself, "But I don't have money to do things with my kids." If you are a single mom, that is very easy to believe. How do some single moms even survive? But there are things to do that don't cost a lot of money. I had every other weekend off from my job. We went through phases, so we didn't do this forever and ever, but for a long time, every other Saturday morning, each of the kids got to choose something they wanted to do.

For the longest time, Noah chose to go to "The Honda Shop" to check out the motorcycles. He loved those little Hondas and I never did come up with the money to buy one for him. We still had fun checking them out. He drew pictures of Honda motorcycles and had them pinned all over his walls. He lived and breathed those bikes. Soon the guys at the shop got to know him by name. "Hey Noah," they'd call out to him when he walked into the store. He carried along his well-worn Honda Brochure and discussed the bikes with the guys. It was at times like these that I wished he had a dad in town or a guy to hang around with.

Just as much as I could predict that my son would choose to go to the Honda Shop, with the same confidence, I could predict that my little daughter would choose to go to the pet store. She loved her little buddies there. She would stare for long periods at the little fish with their beautiful stripes, colors and patterns. They were so beautiful and colorful. She would stare into the tank with her little nose so close to the glass. It seemed like each and every little fish in the tank came up to the glass to say "Hi" and blow lines of bubbles for her. They liked this sweet, gentle little girl with the soft blue eyes and two little blonde ponytails sticking out to the side of her head. All the little critters in there must have known her by name.

We rounded off the morning with a trip to the bakery where we would inevitably make a terrible mess with chocolate and whipped cream (some of us still can't eat a chocolate Eclair without getting stuff all over us and hey, I'm the first to admit it). After our morning out, Saturdays were usually spent splitting wood and moving wood inside to dry. The kids helped of course. Noah and I got to be pretty swift at swinging that axe. When it came to taking care of the wood situation, we were the A-Team. When our chores were done, and if we could afford to, we went out for Pizza. Sometimes we could, sometimes we couldn't (buy Pizza I mean). We learned to be very adaptable when it came to treats.

We did enjoy our Saturday night video though, so we usually stretched for that. If we did not have enough money, we went on a treasure hunt to find all the loose change lying around. The kids took their hot baths, I'd kindle the big wood stove and really get it cooking, then we would snuggle on the couch in our warm comfy jammies. What a good life we had, even if we were all alone. We were the Three Musketeers.

It was real special that we lived by the ocean. It was so much part of our lives that I couldn't readily imagine it not being there. Once when I was back in Ireland, my brother was showing some slides that he had taken over the last year or so. Suddenly there was a picture on the screen that struck me deeply. At first I did not recognize the place or people. The picture was of a huge deep orange sun setting over the ocean. The whole picture was amber and orange. The ocean sparkled with reflections of the huge orange ball bidding it's farewell for yet another day. The foreground was silhouetted against this magnificent ball of fire. On the bleak, deserted bluffs, dark against this awesome sunset, stood a woman. She was holding a tiny little girl with wispy hair on her hip and a little boy held her hand. All three were silhouetted against this feat of nature. They were so together, yet so alone against that huge sky.

My brother was looking at me, waiting for a response. That picture struck a chord in my heart. It took a long time for me to realize that the woman in the picture was me. Those two little kids witnessing that beautiful sunset were my own two little children. That picture summed up a lot of our lives; together, but all alone.

We spent so many happy hours by the ocean. Sometimes we took dinner to the ocean and hung around to watch the sunset. It is such a treat to watch a sunset. As the sun goes down and makes it's glorious exit, we are reminded that the day is over and now we can rest. Tomorrow, when the sun gets up to start the day, we can get up and start our day also. The sun, blue skies and ocean make for a great day and that is where we spent many of ours. Sometimes we went to the tide pools and watched all the little critters enjoy their day. Witnessing life in a tide pool has to be one of the most exciting things that a kid can experience. It fascinates them. It fascinates me and I've seen it many times.

Dorothea and Ivy lived on the bluffs (in a house, of course) and sometimes we went there to fish off the rocks. Noah was a pro. He loved to fish and he had some great catches. When my dad was visiting from

Ireland, we took him fishing at Dorothea and Ivy's. My dad loved to fish also and Noah thoroughly enjoyed teaching his Grandpa how to fish off Dorothea and Ivy's bluffs. I have the sweetest photographs of such an expedition. Dorothea in her seventies, is sitting on the rocks preparing delicacies for the hardworking fishing folk. My dad, in spite of his recent stroke, is out on the rocks reeling in his line. Noah is fishing his little heart out and laughing as usual (Noah in Hebrew means Laughter and he always lived up to his name). And there is my little Suzanne in her Strawberry Shortcake sweats that she loved so much, goofing off, flippantly holding her little fishing pole and hanging out with the men of the house. I'll teach these guys how to fish and have fun at the same time. What a happy bunch we were.

We went camping a lot also. Sometimes every other weekend. It was by no means serious camping. Friday after work, I would load up my little Toyota with packed ice-chest, sleeping bags and chaise lounges. We drove about an hour and a half to M&M campgrounds on Clear Lake. Sometimes we didn't even take a tent. There were bathrooms and showers there. We just slept on the chaise lounges under the stars. It was usually getting dark by the time we arrived.

We placed our so-called beds close to the edge of the lake so that we could hear the little waves lapping. We enjoyed the stars and the moon together and listened to the water, still unsettled from all the boat activity from the day that had just passed. After the kids were tucked in, I would play some old tunes on the guitar and watch the light show put on by the moon playing on the tiny waves. That light show was put on just for me, I know it. It was a wonderful way to end a hectic week. I went to sleep under the moon with my two favorite people sleeping peacefully beside me.

In the morning we woke up, happy that it was Saturday and we were at Clear Lake. It was a long walk, but we meandered in to town to a little greasy spoon cafe. Have you ever noticed how hungry you get when you are camping? We were happy to be eating breakfast, and looked forward to a day spent by the lake with nothing to do but have a good time. We took our time. On the way back to the camp ground, we played on the swings and explored the area. We had a little inflatable raft. Noah, being the male of the group, appointed himself the raft inflator, but we usually took turns at pumping it up. I was nervous with kids around water, so they had to wear a life-jacket at all times. I also put a long rope on the dingy and tied it to the shore. That's O.K., they survived their neurotic mother.

We had nothing to do all day but have fun, and we did. We snacked, we rowed the raft out into the lake and we fished and we went on hikes. In the evening we usually barbecued and roasted marshmallows. Sometimes other friends joined for some part of the weekend and there would be other kids to play with. Either way, we had a good time. Sunday night, I would pull into Dodge with two scruffy, weather-beaten, sleeping kids in the back seat, exhausted from playing and having so much fun in the sun.

Then of course, there were fishing trips with Ivy, the Old Lady of The Sea. I'm so glad that my kids knew someone as wonderful as Ivy. Thank you Lord for bringing Ivy into our lives; our lives were enriched in so many ways. Her little boat is only ten feet and has an outboard motor, but when you are out on the ocean with Ivy, you don't need a better or bigger boat. The thought of being out on that big ocean in a little boat is a little awesome to put it mildly, but when I was with Ivy, I felt safe and secure. Ivy was smart when it came to that big ocean. You see, Ivy is like any good fisherwoman, she loves the ocean and knows it well, but she respects it also. Ivy knew what she was doing and didn't take chances. And so, we had many happy days out there on those big waters in her little boat. Better still, we always came home with lots of fish, and that's what counted to an avid fisherman like Noah. They say that there is enough protein in one fish, to last a man for two days if his body could store it. If our bodies could store it, my kids would have enough protein to last for many days, maybe even years. How many healthy fish dinners we ate, I do not know. I do know that the healthy memories that we shared on Ivy's boat will last a life time.

My mind is so full of happy memories, I have a difficult time figuring out how I had time to work. But I did work of course. I worked a lot. In fact, at the time, I felt that work is all that I ever did. We were not always camping or fishing or hanging out at the beach. We also had busy days filled with earning a living and doing homework. But, our evenings were always special.

There were times when I could not afford a Television. There were also times when I chose not to have a television. Know what happens when there is no television? Well, there is more time for sharing and there is more time for reading. Have you ever noticed that when a television is on, all communication comes to a halt. Today, I was babysitting two little children. We talked for a while, then the Television was turned on. Suddenly these children were spellbound, in a trance, glued to the screen. I looked at the screen and wondered what was so fascinating. I saw nothing, but these children were transfixed. Where did those little children go? They were in another world.

Evenings without television have a lot to offer. Try it and see. In the evenings, we would snuggle up on the couch, in front of a big log fire and read the evening away. Have you ever heard of "Uncle Arthur's Bedtime Stories?" Well, you have now. They are precious and full of wonderful teachings for kids. Each story has a wonderful truth contained in it. Even as an adult, I relished these stories and enjoyed them as much as my kids did. These are stories full of wisdom, teaching children about actions and their consequences, helping kids to make better decisions. We read "Treasure Island" and every evening we looked forward to reading the next chapters. Bedtime was a happy time. We also read books from the library. Those times were so special. Sometimes I wish that we could all huddle on the couch, in front of our big wood burning stove and read for hours. Even as teenagers, my children loved to read.

I know that I have a habit of repeating myself, and I know that this is a repeat, but I have to say it again. It isn't the amount of time that you spend with your kids that matters; it is the quality of time that you spend with them. The listening, the sharing, the special times. It is taking time to teach them special little things and reading their favorite story. It is asking them what special thing they would like to do today and doing it with them. It is holding them close when they feel bad and listening with love as they tell you all about it.

Spend special times with them. Find out the interesting places in your area. Take them to the library and help them find a gold mine in literature. Take them to the pet store to see the little critters or take them to the park where they can climb trees and feed the pigeons. Find a hiking trail nearby where you can go for morning walks. Go on a bike ride. There are so many things to do that do not cost money.

I know that it was easier for me because I have not been subjected to living in a city. I have lived in rural areas where it was easier to find things to do with kids. I live in a small tourist town and there are wonderful places to hike and ride a bicycle. It is not uncommon here to see parents, kids and babies out on bike rides together. It is tougher for those who live in the city, and it is tougher for those who do not have money to spend on recreation. Actually, I can hardly relate to living in an area where these things are not accessible, so you would be quite justified in saying "It's easy for you to talk" I don't know the answer. I just encourage you to find that special retreat for yourself and your kids, even if it is just your own living room. I have a favorite cup that says, "Home is dad's kingdom, mom's world, and a child's paradise".

I wish that every child's home could be his or her paradise. No matter how tough your situation is, spend time with your kids and let them know how precious they are. You may be the only person in the world who communicates this important truth to your child. And don't forget to tell him/her, "You are a wonderful person and I love you with all my heart".

Quality Time - The Ties that Bind

We hear the words "Quality Time" often these days. The words are usually used when marriage or child raising is being discussed. It seems pretty self explanatory. Or is it really? Time spent together with some quality attached to it. But what exactly is quality when it comes to time spent together? Is it fancy expensive vacations or dinner at a fancy restaurant? It could be, especially if we are talking about adults.

To me, quality time is time that renders quality, something of value. In that case I guess, quality time is not the same as a good time. Good quality time, in fact, might be experienced through a difficult and unpleasant time, but a quality time none the less, because you and your child went through it together. Like putting your heads together and figuring out how to deal with the school bully, helping figure out the Math difficulty, or helping them to figure out a plan so that they can do homework and still have time to play.

Now these times may not be fun, but do you see what is happening during these quality times? You and your kids are communicating, sharing, and working as a team. Not to mention, defining a problem, recognizing that problems have solutions, and looking for that solution. Hey, that's a lot of "stuff". That's a whole lot of "good stuff" to have happen just because you spent time with the most important people in your life. Quality Time.

When that little person just isn't acting like herself, and you sense that something isn't quite right, take the time, sit down with her/him, and find out what is wrong. She will probably open up her little heart and tell you. You can love her and start helping her to solve the problem or maybe just listen and allow her to solve the problem.

As we do this, our children learn that we do care about the little things in their lives and above all, they know we are a friend that they can count on, even if we are just a sounding board.

Why do I think that this is all so important? Because, one day soon, those little kids, so adorable and affectionate, will be teenagers. No, I am not saying that teenagers are not adorable. But those adorable kids go through some terrific changes when they become teenagers, even the sweetest of them. They are under a lot of pressure. Pressure from peers, pressure to find independence which usually means pulling away from us.

By the time they become teens, our concerns change. We are not worrying about them getting dirty in the sandbox or playing in the poison oak. Clothes can be washed or replaced, and even though poison oak is uncomfortable, it does go away and there are comfort measures that we can take. Our kids hanging out with the wrong company and experimenting with substances is not as easy to deal with. I am not saying that if we spend time with our kids that they will never step outside the boundaries. I am saying though that open communication is important and that it needs to start when they are little.

If our kids did not come to us with problems when they were little, it is unlikely that they will come to us with problems when they are teenagers. In spite of their struggle for independence, this is possibly the time that they need us most of all. We don't need to be fussing at them or constantly showing our concern for them (so easy to do). Sometimes we have to be quiet and not show our concern, but be there, showing that we believe in them (If this is not a test in faith, I don't know what is), communicating to them that we trust them and know that they will do the right thing.

They need to know that they can come to us when they make a mistake. Once again, this kind of communication needs to start when they are very young. Teenagers will make mistakes. How can they learn the incredible amount of life they have to learning those adolescent years without making wrong choices some of the time? I am an adult and I make so many mistakes. They need to be able to share their failures as well as mistakes. Can your kids come to you and say, "Mom, I blew it." Can your child climb up on your knee and tell you about the "wrong" thing that he did? Are you able to say in return, "What do you think you will do to fix this"? Your child might have to go to someone and apologize or offer to pay for something which was broken. He will learn that you are there for him, there are consequences for wrong actions, and that wrongs can be made right. Above all, kids need to know that making a mistake does not make them a "bad" person, only a very "human" person.

As we spend quality time with our children, loving them, validating their feelings, listening to what they have to say, they grow up knowing their own self-worth, self-esteem intact. Individuals with good self-esteem tend to make better decisions and treat themselves and others with respect. Isn't that what we want for our children?

Children's personalities vary so much, even in the same family. Words that would not phase a child may tear apart a brother who is more sensitive. Some just need extra love and building up. I am not saying that we should not discipline our kids. If we love them we will discipline and teach them right from wrong and that there are consequences for our actions. But discipline should not tear down, or cause guilt or unworthiness. And discipline should never ever mean abuse or violence.

One day, when my son was about six years old, he was playing in his room with a friend. He said to his little friend, "Our moms have to discipline us and make us do things we don't want to do. That's 'cuz if we don't do them we won't be able to keep a job when we grow up."

He certainly does not have a difficult time keeping a job and he loves to work. Responsibility, accountability, consequences, problem solving, time-management, self-discipline, self-control. It's a lot of "stuff", but it's the "stuff" that happens day by day as we take time, make time and spend quality time with our kids. It cannot be bought with money, exciting trips, new Nikes or expensive jeans. It is not the responsibility of the teacher or baby-sitter. It is the responsibility of the parents and it happens mostly in the home. It takes a lot of time and it takes a lot of love. I know you have the love. You can do your utmost to make the time Quality Time.

Provoke Not Your Children

Did you know that the fifth commandment is the first commandment that comes with a promise? "Honor your Father and Mother that your days may be long upon the land which the Lord your God gives you". Have you noticed that the ten commandments are not just a bunch of silly rules that God sat up in the sky and concocted?

Have you noticed how much the commandments are about Cause and Effect? Actually if we take a close look, they are about safe, healthy living. God, the Father (parent), giving us guidelines to stay safe and out of trouble just the way we, as parents, set down guidelines and parameters for our children. Like, "Johnny, if you crawl up on top of the I greenhouse, you could get badly hurt and we would be very sad." or, "John, if you mess around with your neighbor's wife, you might get killed".

Ever notice the way God disciplines with love and doesn't shove things down our throat? Ever. Yes, we see the laws of sowing and reaping at play all around us. Sometimes things happen in our lives that cause us to sit down and re-evaluate our lives, where we are going and what we are doing. Sometimes a person pops into our lives at the most perfect time, just like Clarence being there when James Stewart was ready to jump off the bridge in "It's A Wonderful Life". There are great stories about these so-called chance encounters. I've even had some myself.

Now, you may not believe as I do, that this is divine intervention, but I am sure most of you will agree that all of this does go on in peoples' lives. This intervention goes on in my life, and the point I am making here is that God never slaps me around. He doesn't get me in a corner and shove things down my throat. And He certainly does not say, "Because I said so and I'm the boss. You'll do it because I said so." No, that's not his style and it positively should not be ours either.

Some parents make it almost impossible for children to keep this commandment. It does not say, "Honor your parents if they are kind to you and treat you like a person." We want our children to be obedient and respect us, yet some of us make that real tough for them. When I was little and my dad yelled and swore at me, I was afraid, and there were times that I hated him and would feel so angry at him for making me feel like that inside. I did not have those feelings when my mother caught us being naughty and attempted to paddle our "Hind-ends."

Now this did not happen too often, because we knew that if we got caught we were in big trouble. We knew that our mother meant what she said and I think that we had a healthy respect for her. With my father, it was a little different. I was more afraid and despised the yelling.

There is such a thin line between respect and fear. I respected my mother; I feared my father. The fifth commandment does not include "fathers do not provoke your children to anger," but those words are used later in the scriptures. Can you respect a bully? Could you respect someone that abused you verbally or mentally? Could you respect someone that shoved his beliefs down your throat, humiliated' you on a regular basis or allowed you to have no opinions of your own? I could not. I would consider such a person a bully and feel sorry for him/her, but I would not respect the individual. Yet this is what we expect from our children when we bully them.

It is so easy to push kids over the edge and cause them to be even more rebellious. No, I am not saying that we should not discipline, but that we discipline in love and provoke not our children to anger.

CHAPTER 4

A Time to Plant
Those Who Sew in Tears
Shall Reap in Joy

    For everything there is a season under Heaven. There is a season to plant, and there is a season to reap. The message in this book is to "be not weary in well-doing." There is a verse in the bible which I came across when I first started my journey as a single parent. I did not quite understand the verse, but it did impress me over the years.

    The verse read, "Those who sew in tears shall reap in joy." This verse could speak about and apply to many things, and occasionally it would come to mind and be encouraging during those struggles when the kids were so little. Sometimes life was tough in those early days as we adapted to being alone. But those early days were also when my kids were very young, open, and impressionable.

    Children are an open book. Their minds are like sponges. Their little hearts are so trusting - a fertile garden waiting for seeds to fall. It is during these early years that children learn about love and trust, or the lack of it. What they learn during these first years is what will greatly impact their lives, even as adults. Truths learned during those early years will probably remain with them during their whole lives.

    Recently I was talking to my son who is now twenty. He ended the conversation with, "All the good stuff I know now, you taught me when

I was little". Kids are learning every day of their lives. That important stuff, the stuff that makes them the adults they are, they are learning from day one. They learn it by the way they are held and cared for.

They learn it from the way they are disciplined. They learn it from the way we relate to them and the respect we give them even as we validate them as a real person, no matter how young or tiny they might be.

It is not the responsibility of the babysitter or the teacher to teach values to our children. Yes, they may reinforce the truths we teach, but these values are learned in the home. It isn't easy, is it? The list goes on and on.

We have to care for our kids physically, We have to work hard to meet their needs. We need to keep up with the housework and the laundry. And, it does not end there.

Teaching children about honesty, responsibility, consequences, and how to deal with anger, takes a lot of commitment. It happens on a one to one basis. It happens in our homes as we do our everyday chores. It happens when we snuggle on the couch and read bed-time stories together. It happens when we say prayers together and talk about the events of the day. Nothing can replace that special time we spend with our children.

As the divorce rate increases, so does the number of single parents. Being a parent is not an easy task if we commit ourselves and do the job with all of our hearts. Today, more and more, I hear young single moms say, "This is my time." I also hear single moms say, "But, what about me?" It is all so understandable. They are young. Most of them are young and want to have fun. Some are newly divorced, and want to go out and have a good time now that they are single.

Yet, it strikes a chord in my heart. Mom may be quite justified in wanting to have a good time. She may be tired and overwhelmed by the responsibility, but what about the kids? They did not ask to be brought into this world. This was not their decision. Many of us decided to have children. Perhaps I am extremely old fashioned, but I believe that we do have a responsibility to our children.

For generations, women have raised children and raised few questions. Our mothers made many sacrifices to raise us. They did not sit around and contemplate the sacrifices made to raise us. Many of our mothers placed dreams on the back burner. Some went on to realize their dreams after the children left home. I know that this will not settle well with many single moms out there, but I do believe with all of my heart that our obligation is to our kids.

Our children need us. For many of them, we are all they have. A mom is a very special person in a child's life. Often there is no other close family member. And, what if there is? We, their moms, are who they love so dearly. I'm not saying that we should not have fun sometimes, and that we should not go to school or be committed to our job or business. But, I do believe that our children should be number one priority in our lives.

Raising children is like planting a garden. We sow the seeds and one day we will reap. We need to be there for our kids. They need to know that they are loved, and that they are more important than our friends or career. They may not say this to us, but they look to us for the answers.

It seems like, in the blink of an eye, our children are grown and independent. Time passes so swiftly. Our children grow up as we live our lives. Soon, they will be gone. Soon we will have so much time to do the things we wanted to do. Yes, we can pursue our dreams and miss out on our children growing up. We accomplish our dreams and our kids are gone. Now what do we have?

For years, mothers have placed their dreams on the back burner, married or single. I realize that this can be carried to an extreme. Mothers abandon their own lives for their children, and when the kids are gone, they have nothing to live for. This is sad, but it is not what I am talking about here. I am not saying that we should not go to school, or have interests outside of our children. I am saying though, that our childrens' needs do come first. We need to take care of the job at hand, and that is being there for them.

Yes it is tough, and yes, there are many sacrifices to be made. Like many mothers all over the world though, I will say from my heart. "Be not weary in well-doing. Your time will come. Sew the seeds and reap the harvest".

Your Time Will Come

As single parents, we juggle and we juggle. We juggle from morning to night and we juggle so many balls that our heads spin. Days run into each other, as do the weeks and the years. Our days off whiz by and our evenings whiz by. Sometimes it feels like we are chasing our own tails and getting nowhere fast.

We get up in the morning and whiz through the routine of delivering the kids to the baby-sitter and being at work by seven A.M. After work, we either go to our next job or rush over to pick up the kids. We make a quick stop at the store maybe, hurry home and put the groceries away. Sometimes the kids have an after school activity and we deal with that also.

We organize the kids to do homework, throw in a load of laundry and get dinner rolling. After dinner, we complete homework if necessary, encourage the kids to get everything ready for the morning, and then hopefully, we have some quality time together. When the kids are in bed, we do, or finish the dishes, clean up the kitchen, fold the laundry and put it away. Tomorrow, we start the cycle all over again.

Does any of this sound familiar to you? It was certainly very typical of my life as a single mom. I cannot speak for you, but I know that for me, there were times when I was totally wiped out. There was no one to pick up the slack. If I did not do it, it just did not get done. There were times when I was totally overwhelmed, exhausted and discouraged. This is not a complaint; this was just life as a single mother of two little children.

Maybe I took it all too seriously, but I did not like to go out much and leave the kids. Already we had so little time together and I did not want to leave them anymore than I had to. It seemed that their lives already were mostly spent at babysitters. My time with them was special.

There came a time when they were older, that I thought of taking an aerobics class or a tap dancing class. So often though, I did not have the extra money for daycare. It would only have cost thirty or forty dollars, but there were times when I just did not have the money to spare.

At one point in time, I actually started working on a Bachelor's degree in Nursing. The course was mostly Home study, which eliminated a huge need for day care. I was usually up at five, studying or writing papers. After the kids were tucked in, I would be buried in books again, studying until the wee hours.

I had the type of job where I really had to have my wits about me. Unfortunately, at the same time, I was involved with a man who was also a single parent. I did plan a schedule and tried to stick to it, but, something had to give. Eventually, the degree went by the way side, and over the course of time, so did the relationship. I had enough to juggle as a single parent, working full-time, without all the other demands on my life.

It wasn't a hardship to give up the other things; I really did not have much choice. I was responsible for these children and I thoroughly enjoyed the time devoted to them. This was my reality. I was all they had. As parents, we are sometimes obligated to put things on the back burner. There are many parents who could tell you what I am trying to say. That is, your time does come, and sometimes all too soon.

Why do I take the time to describe a scenario so typical of your own life? Only because I know now especially how quickly that scenario changes. My life is so different now. My son is nineteen and does not live with me. My daughter is almost seventeen. Wow, how life changes. A typical six-teen year old spends a lot of time in her room, and on the phone. Friends become their life. They typically, I believe, grow away from family get-togethers. Camping trips and vacations do not appeal as they used to. All in all, their lives take on a new kind of "busyness".

Yes, we go to the Mall sometimes, and go eat a meal, but usually only if it is part of the trip to the Mall. Again, this is not a complaint. This is reality. Kids grow up and change before our very eyes. Before we know it, instead of them asking us to take them places, we are inviting them to go places with us.

One of my favorite things to do is to go to the ocean. Little kids love trips to the ocean. They play in the water, build sand-castles, write in the sand, get excited over the seals, and spend hours running on the beach. That used to be so much fun. Now, trips to the ocean involve a group of friends. I still go to the ocean quite frequently. Now I go alone. In fact, I do a lot of things alone. I still have to work many hours a week, and I still have lots of housework to keep me busy. But now I have time for hobbies.

I spend hours planting and growing flowers. I take tennis lessons, and workout and fast walk on a regular basis. Now I read, and write, and do so many things I did not have time to do. Your time too will come, and I encourage you to be patient. Spend time with them, and graciously put those things on the back burner. One day, all the "Busyness" will be gone and you will have the opportunity to do the things that you did not have time to do.

You will be glad that you waited. In fact, you will be glad that even though the kids are grown, you still have dreams to work on. Your life will be vital in spite of the "pre-empty nest". For almost fifteen years, it has been on my heart to write about the joys of being a single mom. When the children were little, I had time only to live it, and with all the "hurry and scurry", it seems it has passed in the blink of an eye. Now it is my time, and so many doors are opening up to me.

I have two wonderful children, but I must admit, I miss those two little kids. Life is funny, isn't it? When we are so busy, we wish that we had more time. Then, when we have the time, we miss the "busyness" and those needy little kids. Don't misunderstand me. I do not sit and pine that the kids are growing up and do not need me as much. I just want to tell you what it is like on the other side. I enjoy the time allowed me now, and hopefully I will push open the doors before me. I am a very happy person as I sit here and write.

My trips to the ocean are very enjoyable, and my life is very full of good things. Yours will be some day also. In the meantime, be patient, and be not weary in well doing. Your time will come.

Fill Up the Cup

All through these writings, I have talked so much about giving to our kids. I made many mistakes as I raised my children, and I wish I had known as much when the kids were little as I know now. But, that is not how it works, is it? No, I did not know as much back then. I guess I just kept putting one foot in front of the other and dealing with situations as they arose. I am not putting myself down. I know that I did the best with the knowledge and understanding that I had at the time, and strangely enough, we all survived.

As a nurse I hear the word "burnout" used frequently. I personally have experienced "burnout" quite severely in nursing. Books could be written on the subject. What causes "burnout?" To me, burnout is a condition where we give and give and do not replenish the cup. We pour ourselves out of the cup, but we don't have or make the time to fill up the cup. The cup becomes empty. The demands and the need to give are still there, but now it seems, we just do not have it to give anymore.

Does this sound familiar to you as a single parent? Our lives are so full of busyness and taking care of other people. I know a lot of single moms who are also care-givers. Giving comes so easily to us. It is like second nature. Have you ever noticed how much we give to other people, and yet how difficult it is to spend time on ourselves?

Most of us, as single parents, do not have time or money to go to the and have a massage (nice dream, right?). We work until we fall into bed. Yes, on our days off, we spend time with the kids, and those are good times, but when do we fill up the cup? How do we fill up the cup?

This was possibly my weakest area as a single parent. In fact, not just as a single parent, but as an individual. I guess I was more of a Tomboy growing up. All in all, I was not very feminine. Make-up, forget it. I would rather ride horses and go hiking, than deal with any of that stuff. Make-up and dressing up was a royal pain to me.

Now, I have a teenaged daughter who could write articles on beauty tips. What is surprising is that so many kids today know how to take care of themselves. Now maybe you all did also, but I must admit I did not have a clue.

How do you fill up your cup on your day off, or after a hectic week? What fills you and inspires you? How well do you take care of yourself? It does not have to cost a lot of money. Libraries are free. I used to say that once a week, I was going to treat myself to a nice hot bubble bath and spoil myself. You know, it seldom happened. Months would go by, and I would not take the time. Today, I have much more time to relax and I am learning to do it better. It would have helped back then when everything was so much more hectic. Now I realize the importance of exercise, which in itself reduces stress. In fact, working out and fast walking on a regular basis has significantly lowered the stress level in my life.

It is so easy to get on a roll and never slow down. I write about this to encourage you to take the time to fill up the cup. Only you know how to do this and what works for you.

Whatever that something is, make the time to do it. I wrote about making time to spend time with the kids. It is just as important to make time to spend on yourself. It is so important. If we do not take time out to replenish the cup, we burn out, become irritable and discouraged. Our kids do not need this. We can maintain, and we can keep up the good work, but only if we make the time for ourselves also.

Perhaps you enjoy long walks, or just window shopping. Why not work out a deal with a friend, to let the kids play for a couple of hours each week and have fun, while you both take turns at doing your favorite thing. My treat back then was to walk on the beach. I loved to take my kids to the beach, but it was a real treat to go to the beach alone sometimes. I found that when I was by the ocean, I could write poetry, and that made me very happy. I used to long for the opportunity to go to the beach alone but it didn't happen often. Later, when the kids were in school, and I had a day off, I would make a serious effort to take time away from housework and go to the beach for an hour or so. When the kids were with their father on holidays, I would have many hours to spend by the ocean, but then I was torn because they were gone for so long and I missed them so much.

Single parents have an incredible challenge to overcome. It can be done, because many have done it before us and lived to tell the tale. But, it can be a sad and lonely road at times. We love our kids, and giving does not seem like a sacrifice Keep in mind though, the empty cup, and see to it that it is filled and replenished. Find out what replenishes your cup and fill it on a regular basis. If the cup is dry we and our children may experience a drought.

How Do You Spell Relax?

As I have said before, I was not, and am not, good at relaxing. In fact, my times of relaxation were so infrequent, that I remember them well. They were very special to me and now are very much part of my life. What was a treat then is normal now, but none the less, very enjoyable.

We lived in a double-wide trailer, on an acre out in the woods. I enjoyed our lives there so much and still miss those happy times alone, together. Our little home was humble and very cozy. I did not have much money to spend on extra things, but I did love to grow flowers and plants. Many happy hours were spent creatively (without money) landscaping our wild acre out in the forest. Creating a little home was my hobby, and many an evening I was out on the covered deck planting seeds, which I would transplant in the spring.

Winters were long in Fort Bragg, and often there was storm after storm. Sometimes I love to walk in the rain and get really wet. Then it feels good to take a hot shower, put on some sweats and look out the window at the rain falling down so hard. Sometimes the sound of the rain was so loud falling on the trailer roof.

I miss it sometimes, that warm cozy feeling I mean. We had a big wood-burning stove that glowed and put out so much heat. MMMMM, was it cozy. We would be toasty warm inside and listen to the rain pounding on the trailer roof. Those were the nights we huddled on the couch, in front of the stove and read. Sometimes I want to move back there just to experience that warm toasty feeling. We were together and happy.

One Saturday, I went to an all day class with other staff from the hospital where I worked. On a break, people were talking about their plans for their Saturday evening. Someone asked what my plans were. I said, "I'll watch a movie with the kids. Then when they are in bed, I will read and sit in front of the fire". They thought I was nuts. At the time, I was working the evening shift from three P.M. until eleven thirty P.M. So it was a treat to be home with the kids.

Yes, this was my idea of a treat. When the kids were tucked in, I would sit in front of the fire and listen to classical music. This was a treat in itself, but it got better. I would read or knit. All of my favorite things squeezed into one evening, and I would sit up late enjoying every minute of it all. It was so seldom that I had time to knit or read. On these rare occasions, I would listen to Beethoven, enjoy the fire and knit or read 'till my heart was content.

This is how I spelt "Relax" and it was a treat worth waiting for. It may not be your cup of tea, but find something that brings you great satisfaction and do it for a special treat. After this, I could face any hectic week and look forward to the time when I could enjoy my treat again.

Weekends are still special to me because I work hard Monday through Friday. I do not have a wood burning stove, but I still spend most weekend evenings alone and still love to listen to classical music and read. In fact, last weekend I did not write much and instead read "Pride And Prejudice". I could not stop reading.

One day, I want to live in a little cabin by the ocean. In the winter I will enjoy the sound of the wind and the rain, and will even go for walks along the beach in the rain. I will light a fire, watch the rain failing and listen to classical music. I will knit and read and write and be very thankful for many blessings.

Early this year, I was working very long hours and driving two hours a day. When the goal was accomplished, I managed to take a week-end off. I rented a cabin in Mendocino, close to the ocean. The after-noon was spent by the ocean writing, something I had not done for a long time. I lit a blazing fire when I returned to the cabin. It was like old times and about fifteen miles from where I had lived. I could have stayed with friends, but I just needed some time alone.

That evening, I sat in front of the fire and read with Beethoven playing in the background. It was so quiet and peaceful. In the morning I went to the coffee shop in Mendocino for a latte, then went to my friend's house. She and her husband are wonderful friends. We spent the day horseback riding through the woods. It was a glorious ride. The flowers were starting to bloom and everything was still green from the winter rains. The sun was warm and the creeks were full and flowing. It was a wonderful treat after five months of hard work, and my feet were walking on air as I drove south to start yet another week of work.

How do you spell RELAX? These treats do not have to happen every day, but these treats can keep us moving ahead for a long time. In fact, when I finish writing, I am going for a repeat.

A Well Dressed Cabbage Patch Kid

So far I haven't mentioned the other kid in our home. His name was Jonathon and he was very much part of our family. He was probably the best dressed Cabbage Patch kid in town. He suited his name and had dark brown curly hair. Wherever we went, Jonathon went with us. We never had the heart to leave him at home, and Suzanne would never have allowed such a thing to happen.

I do have pictures of Jonathon with the other kids, but better still, I actually have a painting of him. My pastor's wife was a wonderful lady: an artist and a decorator. She was the friend who came to my home one day while I was at work, and transformed our little home with curtains and other hand-made things. That day, she brought with her, a large painting of a little girl kneeling with her dolls and special things around her. The little girl in the painting was obviously Suzanne with her long thick blonde hair, and lying against her knee is Jonathon.

It is a beautiful painting that portrays peace and happiness. The little girl is absorbed in her world and Jonathon is lying by her smiling.

Yes, he was a well loved boy. If how Suzanne cared for her dolls is an indicator of the mother she will be, my grandchildren will have a wonderful mom.

Bonnie was also a seamstress. She made beautiful dresses for Suzanne, and she also made clothes for Jonathon out of left over fabric. He had striped velour pajamas and for Christmas received regular P.J.'s with a collar and fasteners.

Once, I knit a hooded sweater for Jonathon. It was red, had a white stripe on the bottom and sleeves, and had a zipper up the front of it. Then I made corduroy pants to go with it. Suzanne of course made clothes for him also. So believe me, he was a well dressed kid. I still have Jonathon, but better still, I have the memories.

I used to knit little sweaters for the kids also, and they loved their sweaters handmade by mom. These days, hand knit sweaters would not be welcomed; only sweatshirts are acceptable, but I know one day that will change and she will appreciate hand knit sweaters from mom.

Hopefully my kids will not have children for a while. Hopefully they will enjoy their youth before they make such a commitment, but I do look forward to knitting cute little sweaters for my grandchildren. Maybe they will love their babies as much as Suzanne loved Jonathon, and I will knit matching sweaters for their babies.

It's funny. I often listened to older folks say, "I am looking forward to keeping my grandchildren. The nice thing about it is, you can love them and spoil them, then send them home to their parents". Now I know that I am getting old. I certainly do not want to start over and raise children, but already, I am looking forward to loving my grandchildren, doing special things for them just as doting grandmas do, feeling the joy of sharing them and enjoying their company. I know already though that I will feel like those other older folks, and enjoy waving goodbye and looking forward to seeing them again.

P.S. The late forties are wonderful years. Life does just keep on getting better by the year.

We Shall Reap with Joy

Many years have passed since I started my journey as a single mom. It has been seventeen years to the month. Yes, there were some tears shed. Sometimes I wonder how my kids ever survived me. I had such a long way to go and still do. But they did survive. We all did.

There were lots of things that I may have done wrong, but we had one big plus to our lives, and that was love. We were so together. Nothing came between us. They were number one in my life.

We prayed together and we spent hours reading together. We split wood together and hung out on the beach together. Although we were surrounded by friends who cared, I was very aware that I was all they really had. Yes, other people loved them, their needs may be met at a babysitters, but I was their mom, and I wanted to be there for them. I enjoyed being with them. I don't remember a time when I felt that I needed to escape from them. Our time together was special.

Yes, I did often wish there was more time in a day. Time to do the things I enjoyed, like knitting and reading. Time to sit in front of the fire and read a magazine without nodding off to sleep. But these were small sacrifices. Always I was aware that they were growing up so fast.

And they did. My son is twenty and my daughter is in her final year of high school. Soon she will leave also. And I am so happy that I took the time to enjoy them when they were little. I have great memories of the time we spent together have no regrets about the time and love I shared with them.

It is hard to believe that they are grown, and oh, do I my miss those little kids my wee bairns. I still hear their laughter and pleas for more stories. I remember Suzanne's total dedication to her own babies, and Noah's never-ending excitement about life, and his infectious laugh. I remember those cozy evenings with the light from the log fire, as we snuggled on the couch with our down quilt. I remember the prolonged sweet Good-nights when they manipulated their mom so that they could stay awake just a little longer.

I wouldn't change those memories for anything. And yes, in the beginning I may have "sowed in tears", but today I reap with joy. I say joy, because I love what and who those two little kids are today.

I'm glad that I put things on the back burner. Soon it will be my time, and I have lots of plans. I've worked hard these last seventeen years without regret. I've often done work that I did not enjoy, and even though it is against my philosophy, I did it because it was necessary at the time.

Now I know what I want to do in life. It will mean going back to school, but soon I will have the opportunity to do just that. There was not time when the kids were little, but now there is time. I cannot imagine living alone without Suzanne. I know that I will miss her the same as I miss Noah. But, I have a very full life ahead with great plans.

I'm glad that I was too busy to write when the kids were little. Now I have lots to write about. I'm glad that I devoted myself to them when they were young and needed me. Now I have the rest of my life to pursue my dreams which I tucked away years ago. Isn't life exciting?

Enjoy your kids when they are little. Sew the seeds and reap a wonderful harvest. Your time will come.

Chapter 5

A Time to Love

    A couple of weeks ago, I was discussing this book with a publisher. I asked for some constructive criticism on the manuscript. She said, "It's a success story. T.V. is swamped with success stories." I had a real chuckle to myself. A success story. It felt very hilarious, because I was really and truly broke. I felt that after seventeen years, I was back to square one.

    I knew that what she was talking about was success in raising two children alone as a single mom. She said, "What did you do right? What did you do wrong? What did you teach your kids? What did your kids teach you?" That folks was a question which required some thought, and I actually thought that a lot of those answers were already in what I had written.

    Most of the credit is due my children themselves. It seems to me that they are individuals who know who they are and what they want. Yes, they are far from perfect, just as I am, but they are good people. They have their own personalities and characteristics, and they are strong. My son is extremely independent. He has excellent work ethics, sometimes works two jobs and is self-sufficient. My daughter knows very much what she believes. She is not interested in academics, but has a great flair for writing. She is five feet tall, although she will be eighteen in December. She may be small in stature, but she is a very determined individual.

    Noah was born happy, just like his name. As a child he was always so enthusiastic about life. He loved facts as his dad did, and he loved to learn. I remember waking up one Sunday morning. I could hear Suzanne giggle occasionally and say the name of a state Capital. Noah was his usual excited self, and totally into his endeavor. He was probably about six and Suzanne about, three. He was enthusiastically trying to teach her the Capitals of every State. She was trying, because she did love her big brother. I just lay in bed and chuckled.

He used to get so absorbed in hobbies. He loved football, and he would draw football helmets of all of the teams (I did try hard to learn them). Then he would tape them up all over his bedroom walls. If it wasn't that, it was Honda Motorcycles. One day, he said to me, "Mom, I get so fanatical about things." Yes he did. He was so enthusiastic about everything, even having fun.

Suzanne was happy also, but she was a lot quieter. She was very easy-going and loving. She loved her babies and animals, and she loved her mom so much. She was very close to me. She was such a contented kid, and she would sit and play alone for hours.

She was so tiny. On her first birthday, she weighed nineteen pounds. Her little legs were so short. Yes she was a sweet child and she did not get upset easily. I remember the first time I saw her really upset.

Suzanne, Noah, grandma and myself were playing "Hide the Button." Noah was having a great old time, being rambunctious, and taking advantage of his little sis who was so tiny and good-natured. He was telling her that she was hot when she was cold, and that she was cold when she was hot. She told him to stop and he just laughed. Well, the scenario which followed, left all of us with our mouths hanging open, and Noah's eyes as big as saucers. She eyed him from across the room (I remember she was wearing fluffy sleepers and looked like a sweet little Bunny rabbit). Those legs may have been short, but they moved at a deadly pace across the living room. She ran to Noah and pounded him.

We were in shock. It all happened so fast and the look of terror on Noah's face was a sight to behold. The whole incident was a sight to behold. I held my breath. Of course I took care of the situation. My mother and I both ran to Noah's rescue. I looked at my mother and had this incredible urge to laugh. I was ready to explode. I had to turn my face away. Noah gained his composure quickly and then he found the situation funny also.

We didn't laugh in front of Suzanne. I did all of the "mom" things and mentioned how we couldn't attack people. But deep down we were all so proud of her. She had enough of this. Noah did not tease her as much after that, and many a laugh we've had when we looked back on it. Those little legs a'running, and those little fists a'pounding.

It was a touchy subject and one I dealt with the best way I knew possible. Our children need to know that it is O.K. to stand up for themselves. It is O.K. to be angry, but we need to deal with our feelings, and violence is not the answer.

My mother gave me some very good advice when Suzanne was little. In fact, it may have been right after this incident. She said, "Sarah, don't break this child's spirit. She is small for her age, and she is female. She'll need all of that spunk and determination." Suzanne did stay very small for her age. When she was five, she looked like she was about three. She looked like a little doll and kids her own age tended to baby her. When they played "House," she always had to be the baby. She often grew tired of that.

Being inches and inches shorter than your peers is not much fun. I had the same problem to deal with when I was a kid, so I know how it feels. How do we raise children and discipline them without breaking their spirit? How do we teach right from wrong without damaging their self-esteem?

I am glad that my mother gave me her advice. Sometimes though, when my daughter and I lock horns, and she is determined, I say to myself, "O.K. mom, you gave me the advice. Now you can come and deal with it." But I really don't mean it. Determination in our lives is usually a real plus. Without determination my mother could not have done what she did. Without determination I could not have done what I have done so far in my life. My daughter is determined, and with some refinement, that determination will take her a long way.

I've shared these stories to tell you that I cannot take all of the credit for how my children are. Like any one born into this world, they were special little individuals with gifts and personalities of their own. I was pretty wiped out when I first started raising them alone. I was a typical mom, grouchy and irritable at times. I lost my cool sometimes and did not handle situations well. I was often stressed and probably over-reacted way more than I should have.

One thing I do know though, I loved these kids so much. Raising them in a loving environment was the priority in my life. Being with them as much as possible and sharing in their lives was of utmost importance. I was keenly aware that it was the three of us alone, together. I knew that no-one would ever love them as much as I did, and that no-one could care for them as I did.

I was so aware that the words that came out of my mouth could tear them down or build them up, and that how I taught them and disciplined them could affect their self esteem and their own self worth. I did not want them to hurt as I had hurt.

There were possibly times when I may have been inadequate. I had so much to learn myself. It is said that "love covers a multitude of sins." I believe that love is always the answer. Love was the motivation behind our lives. Maybe I was altogether weird, but I did not want to go out and leave them any more than I had to. I could have worked more than forty hours a week and made some extra money, but chose to manage with less money, and go without some things, so that I could be with them.

Yes, there was a lot of love in our happy little home. We did not have much, but we had each other. Together we were strong, growing and learning together.

To everything there is a season under Heaven. A time to love----Always it is the season to love our children. When they are little, is the time to love them with all of our hearts and plant seeds of love.

Praise Works

It's so easy to fall into the trap of criticizing our children, especially when we are tired and over-wrought. When we criticize our children, we put them on the defensive - we make ourselves the enemy. Kids perform much better when they receive praise.

When we praise our children, we are focusing on the positive and encouraging them to do better. None of us want to be reminded constantly of our faults. We know they are there. How much better we perform when we are praised. We are thrilled that we are appreciated and strive to do better.

Recently, I had the pleasure of working for a boss who really appreciated me. As an adult, I have learned to do my job without praise, and in fact if my performance depended on praise I wouldn't accomplish much. A lot of managers have not yet learned that praise works (and they need to). This job was quite an undertaking. I could have done the job without all of the praise, but it was a treat to work for someone who believed in me as much as this person did.

I trusted this person and made the mistake of being human. I had worked long days for about six months, but during that time goals had been reached. We passed with flying colors. However, I had made a boo-boo. I made myself vulnerable and complained about being tired. Tables turned and now I received not praise, but criticism. Nothing was ever good enough and instead of hearing praise I heard ultimatums. I could have done the job without praise, but it was tough to do the job with ultimatums. In fact, I don't do well with ultimatums. I left.

Have you ever praised your child and noticed how their attitude changes? Try it and see; you'll be amazed. Many times I fell into the trap of being frustrated with my kids and criticizing them, and nagging. The results were pretty negative. Nagging, what a losing game that is. King Solomon, in Proverbs, talks about nagging. He went as far as to say, "It is better to dwell in a corner of a housetop, than with a brawling woman in a wide house." Have you ever been nagged. You stand there and just listen, feeling totally defeated.

As I said, I would fall into the trap of nagging. Usually I was pulled up short. I could just look at them and see what criticism was doing to them. Then, instead of criticizing them, I would love them, appreciate them and focus on all the good things that they did. Before I knew it, peace was restored and things were back to normal. Criticism does not work. If we have to discipline, we do that, and it is over with. It is settled, and we do not continue to criticize.

Criticism only serves to tear down and focus on the negative. Praise builds up and restores. Praise builds confidence and self-esteem. Our praise should not be phony either. Kids see through that. When my son was very, very little, he was not good at sports. I felt bad because I wasn't the best person to get out there and teach him how to pitch a baseball (I didn't have a clue). I played ball with him, but he did not run fast. I'd say, "Honey, you're doin' better." My heart went out to him.

Sometimes we talked about it. I remember saying, "Noah, I know that little boys want to be good at baseball, but look at all the other things you are good at. You are the smartest little boy I know". And he was. I would point out to him all the things that he was so good at. One day he said to me, "Mom, I know that I'm not good at sports, but that's O.K., I'm good at other things". He told me some things that he was good at, and this mom had a happy heart. He had come to terms with it, but I don't think that he felt inferior that he was not a prize athlete.

I feel that we are at liberty to praise our children for every effort they make. I wasn't very good with messes, but I tried. Sometimes the kids wanted to do the dishes - in fact, sometimes they argued about who would do the dishes. I suggested that they take turns washing and drying (I knew that it wouldn't last long). They played in the water and washed the dishes. I remember little peanut and her brother slaving over the kitchen sink with their aprons on. I'd go to the kitchen and tell them that they were the best little dish washers a mom could wish for. They worked so hard.

They were probably only about two and four at the time and they loved being mom's little helpers. When they were tucked into bed, mom would clean up the kitchen. Yes, they were good little-dishwashers and good little sweepers. They were also great little vacuumers and window cleaners. They made super sandwiches (especially peanut butter and jelly) and best of all they gave the best hugs in the whole wide world.

Hey, It's only a Game

Just a few days ago, I came across a photograph of Suzanne's soccer team. Eight smiling kids in their soccer outfits. There she stands in the front row, inches shorter than all the other kids, pig tails and bobbles, and a smile that says, "I am so happy to be here".

I also have photographs of her in an album, wearing her soccer gear. She is standing with her back to the camera, showing off her number. Underneath I wrote, "Watch out Georgie Best, here I come." Not being a spectator sports fan, Georgie Best was the only name I could come up with, because he was a famous soccer player when I was a kid in Ireland.

Soccer is a great game and the average kid in Ireland grew up kicking a ball around. I forget the history of soccer, but it did evolve as a sport because kids enjoy kicking. If there wasn't a ball available kids found something else that could be kicked and we spent many happy hours kicking a can around. It wasn't competitive, just plain old fun.

Anyway, this talented group of kids practiced for weeks and finally the games started. What better way to spend a Saturday morning than watching five and six year old kids, in bright colors play a fun game? My father was visiting from Ireland and as usual had his infamous video camera in tow (He used to be very sneaky with his camera, and I was always looking over my shoulder to see what he was up to).

Anyway, it was yet another beautiful, blue sky day along the coast and we were glad to be there watching the kids play soccer. Little Peanut was by far the smallest kid out there on the soccer field. Most of the time there was not much action around her area. My father was having a super time videotaping the kids and of course couldn't wait to get some action from his little granddaughter on tape. Finally his opportunity arrived because the ball was kicked over to Peanut.

The soccer ball, higher than her little knees, rested by her feet. Parents started to yell out and become upset. I called out to her, "Suzanne, kick the ball". What I failed to do was tell her which direction to kick the ball. The crowd was upset and continued to yell. Eventually she did kick the ball, but unfortunately kicked it in the wrong direction. After all, the ball was in front of her and she was told to kick. What an uproar she caused. I laughed and my father had the whole scene on tape.

My father, my son and I laughed, but the rest of the spectators did not laugh. They took the whole game so seriously. The video camera had sound and picked up what was said around us, including the obscenities. I was shocked and commented about how adults could take a soccer game for five and six year olds so seriously. The whole experience was an eye opener for me and made me sadder than anything else.

Why do we do this to our children? Sports are supposed to be fun. In sports kids learn to be team players. When Suzanne played soccer, she was about the size of a three year old. She was so happy to be there and she did not even know that she had committed such a terrible crime. That day I saw other children put under such unnecessary pressure by adults, not by each other. Left alone they probably would have had a good time.

Sometimes parents put great pressure on children to succeed. There is a big difference between pressure and encouragement. So often parents who feel that they have failed, expect their dreams to be lived out through their kids. We have all seen this undoubtedly. If our children are to be fulfilled as individuals, they need to find out their talents and use them. Their being what we want them to become will not bring into their lives, the happiness and fulfillment which is rightfully theirs. They cannot live our dreams, they must live their own.

There are so many professional people who are unhappy because they were pushed by parents into a particular profession. Peanut did not become a Georgie Best and, in fact, does not enjoy participation in sports. My son is very smart but I cannot choose a profession for him. My daughter has a flair for writing and I hope that she goes on to use her talent but I must not push her. In my heart I say, "Honey, don't make poor decisions as I did and not have the opportunity to write until you are almost fifty".

Our children do need guidance and encouragement, especially to work in school, but we need to remember also that they are children. They need to play and have fun. They need to be allowed to be children.

My father showed off his video tapes at home in Ireland and I hear they loved the soccer game. I can just see my sisters laugh hysterically at the cute little kid looking around at those crazy adults and then kick the ball just as she was told to do I bet they rolled on the floor. After I found the soccer photograph, I asked Suzanne if she remembered kicking the ball toward the wrong goalie. She did and she laughed.

Merry Christmas Noah

My son was an adorable child (all of us parents think that). I was in a very unhappy marriage and this child was what kept me going. I was very aware of that, so I strove to not let my love for him be an unhealthy one. That would have been easy to do because he was the dearest person in my whole life.

When Suzanne was born, Noah was two and a half years old and my marriage was truly on the rocks. It was a very sad time in my life. I was giving birth to a second child, and what did I have to offer her? My life was in turmoil and my heart was truly breaking. She was born December twenty-third and it was possibly the saddest night of my life. I wasn't sad about having this beautiful little child, but the circumstances were so difficult and I was shattered beyond words.

It was almost Christmas and I was about to give birth. I wanted so much to be close to friends who loved me and cared about me. I was homesick and very lonely. Just two days before, I had a doctor's appointment. My doctor told me that he had made a mistake, this baby was not due until February. My reply was, "No, this baby will be born before Christmas." I knew it in my heart and I can't explain why, as women we know these things.

I made it to the hospital just in time to deliver her and my heart was heavy with grief. The nurse handed her to me. She nursed, fell asleep on my chest and together we slept and bonded. She was tiny because she was born prematurely, but she was healthy and feisty.

I missed my little son, but I went home the day after Suzanne was born. The ladies from the Hospital Auxiliary had made these adorable Christmas Stockings for babies born in the hospital around Christmas time. They were made out of soft red flannel, with a deep red and white cuff and the baby fitted snugly inside. So, I took tiny baby Suzanne home in a Christmas stocking (I still have it).

Noah was waiting at home to see his little sister. He was so happy to have his own little baby. He was sitting on the couch waiting to hold her all by himself. I placed her on his knee and said, "Merry Christmas Noah! This is your Christmas present, your very own little baby". He was so happy! He held her in her little Christmas stocking and just looked at her. From then on, he claimed that she was his baby.

One day, many years later when I was raising the kids alone, the principal of the school called me. She was concerned about Noah. My heart sank. Noah was on the honor roll and could certainly afford to get involved in extracurricular activities, yet he had a difficult time getting involved in other things. He seemed too responsible. I talked to him about this when he came home from school. He said, "Mom, I can't help it. I always feel that I need to be checking on Suzanne. I always want to make sure that she is safe".

I felt so bad. In fact, I felt like a total failure. What had I done to my son to give him this over sense of responsibility? What had I done to lead him to believe that he was responsible for his little sister every minute of his life? To be truthful, I did have a lot of fears about leaving my kids at times (a lot of the time). Had I somehow transferred this fear to him? I still don't know the answer.

I explained to him that I appreciated his love and concern for his little sister, but that he could not be responsible for her twenty-four hours a day. He appeared to be somewhat relieved. I know that he continued to be her big brother, but I believe that he ceased to be her care taker.

Maybe he took me literally when I said that this was his baby. I really don't know. He was much too young to be carrying a burden like that. He will know that burden soon enough when he has his own children.

Laughter Turns To Tears

My son was the happiest, bubbliest baby I knew. I sometimes called him "Bubbles" because he was so bubbly. I have a baby album of Noah and in every photo he is laughing and happy. He did not cry much and that was a God send, because my life was not very favorable at the time. He went to bed every night at seven and he loved to sleep. Each night we would have fun together and then go through our bed-time ritual. I carried him around his room and we would say good-night to lots of things. We said good-night to his Paddy-bear (It came from his Grandma in Ireland, so it was a Paddy-bear instead of a Teddy-bear), we said good-night to his Winnie The Pooh light, and we even said good-night to his Winnie The Pooh curtains. He laid down happily and went to sleep.

He had a nap every day at ten A.M. and two P.M. When he woke up, I could hear him laugh and talk to himself. Yes, he was a happy baby. He was my little gift of laughter and sunshine. Noah continued to be a happy little boy through all the hard times.

There came a time though, when my son did not laugh as much. It seemed that he cried so much. He was about seven ears old. I was so busy and stressed and it seemed that this poor kid just cried about so little. I had some well-meaning friends who advised me to put an end to the crying. I tried to be firm with him, but in my heart I was not happy. I knew my child and I knew that he did not cry without reason.

I worked with an MD who was a very special caring person. It seemed like I was always telling him my problems even when I did not want to. One day I met him in the corridor and he asked how I was doing. I could have said, "I'm fine," but instead, told him about my son crying and how everything I had tried did not work. He gave me wonderful advice as usual. He said, "Sarah, most kids have two parents. I know that you love your kids. If you can, love them twice as much". This was some of the best advice I ever received.

Yes, I did love my kids very much, and I was exhausted. Even then, I was so aware that I could not be a father to them and it was hopeless to even try. His advice gave me a lot to think about. I went home that day and it wasn't much later that I had an opportunity to put the advice to practice. My son started to cry and I had no idea what he was crying about. This time, I did not take the first advice, I took the advice of my friend whose opinion and advice I respected so much.

Before, I was frustrated by the tears. Instead of being concerned about my son's feelings I had been more concerned, I guess, about how it looked. When my son cried, I lifted him on to my knee and said, "Sweetheart, why are you really crying?" I was totally unprepared at how easily the answer came. It was as if he had wanted to tell me all along if I had only asked. Amidst his tears, he said, "Dan has his dad to take him fishing, John has his dad to take him fishing. I don't have anyone to take me fishing."

All it took was a little TLC and out it all came. He finally had the opportunity to unload what had been troubling him. I felt that my heart had been ripped out of my body. I felt his pain so deeply and I did not have an answer for him. What could I say to comfort him? I could take him fishing, but fishing was not the issue here. He wanted a man around and I could not magically produce one for him.

The crying stopped immediately. The problem was not solved but at least his feelings were validated. I took my friend's advice and tried to love the kids twice as much. Most of all, I learned an invaluable lesson. Sometimes kids feel bad and cannot express their feelings. Sometimes they do not even know why they feel bad inside and it is at this time, that we need to help them get in touch with their feelings. They do not always know why they-do the things they do.

Children were meant to have the love of two parents. Often the children of single parents only have the love of one parent. The demands of single parenting are already great. Can it be that we have to love our children even more? It all seems so overwhelming. We give so much; how can we give more? I don't know the answer. I just know that the need is often great. The task of raising children alone seems almost impossible at times. We, as our understanding increases, somehow, somewhere, find a way to meet those needs. We are strong and we continue to grow stronger.

We don't find all the answers, or I certainly did not. I could not be the person that my son wanted in his life, and that sadness remained with me. I tried to make it up to him, but I could not change the circumstances.

My son does have a father. Many young boys in our country are growing up never having a dad and never having the influence of a father in their lives. Single fathers with children are becoming more common in our society. What about those young girls who grow up without the love and influence of a mother? It is all so sad. Divorce rates continue to rise and consequently the number of single parents rises also.

We work so hard as single parents to give our children the love they need and deserve. So often it is healthier for a child to be raised by a single parent than to grow up in an environment where there is violence and abuse. Still in my heart, I wish that there was no such thing as a child growing up without two parents to love him or her. I wish that there was no such thing as divorce or unwed moms. I just wish that every child in this world could be raised by two wonderful, healthy parents.

This ideal world does not exist, so, in the meantime I encourage you to keep loving your kids. Your reward will be great.

P.S. If your bubbly little kid stops laughing, don't be afraid to find out why. Your heart might hurt, but he needs to tell you how he feels. Little boys need a man to look up to (and don't forget those little girls either).

Love Never Fails

It would be crazy for me to start and tell you how to raise your children. I am not an expert and have had no education about how to raise children. I found myself alone, very far from home, very needy, and I did the best I could with the knowledge I had.

One thing I did know was that I loved my kids and I wanted the very best for them. I was also aware, because of what I had learned about myself, and others with whom I was aquatinted, that what happened in their lives as children would greatly affect their lives as adults, and how they perceived themselves.

I was very human, and had no experience in raising children. But the bottom line was love, and love never fails. "For though I speak with the tongues of men and of angels and have not love, I become as sounding brass or a tinkling cymbal, "Yes, we can tell our children that we love them, but our actions speak louder than words".

I haven't discussed this with my children. They lived through my "Boo-boos, "but hopefully they know that I cared and that I was always there for them. I hope that they know they were number one in my life.

I remember once, while the kids were at a family get-together I spoke to my children's aunt on the phone. I had not had any contact with the family, except with their father. She said, "Sarah, you're doing a great job with the kids. You can tell being around them that they are well loved." That was a real encouragement to me. They were well loved, and it showed.

I shared the preceding stories for a reason. I am not an expert in raising children, but I am able to share with you, what I experienced.

Sometimes, even as adults, we go through periods of frustration and some unhappiness. A lot of time, even adults do not take the time to look inside and see what the problem is. Has that ever happened in your life? Kids are like that also. Sometimes they are just unhappy and do not even know why. We can really help our children to look at why they are unhappy (we also need to learn to do this as adults).

Recognizing a problem and identifying our feelings is more than half of the battle won. Looking at feelings and being able to talk about them, is a real win situation. We need to help our kids to do this. There is so much necessary emphasis on communication today, and it is just as needed with our kids as it is in other relationships.

I could not provide Noah with the person in his life, but at least he was able to talk about what was on his mind. If the principal of the school, who was also a friend, had not called perhaps he would have continued to carry the load of feeling responsible for his little sister. Until we talked about it, I had no idea that he was carrying such a heavy burden.

When they feel bad or are acting out of character, we need to find out what is going on in their tiny little heads. All behavior is meaningful. As adults we act out sometimes and children are not any different.

Sometimes we can inadvertently provoke our children. There have been a few times in these recent years, dealing with a teenager, that I have been driven to the point where I have had to say, "Because I am the parent in this situation and this is how it needs to be." It has not happened often. Yes, they need to know that we are the parents, and we will have the final say, but we do not have to be bullies and dogmatic. Even as adults, we do not particularly like to be ordered to do something because the boss said so.

Kids, like adults, do better with explanations. They are usually able to understand our reasoning. They need to know why certain things are O.K. and certain things are not. They are people also, and when we treat them with respect, they in turn learn to treat themselves and others with respect.

There is a balance required. In some situations, we address them as little adults and respect them as individuals, and yet we still need to allow them to be little kids having a lot of fun.

Sometimes, we as parents, because of our own insecurities, push our kids to be Super kids. Some kids are involved in so many extracurricular activities that they do not have time to play. Kids need time to play and be creative. They need time to use their imagination. They need to kill the dragon and be a hero and be winners. In their adult lives, they will be faced with many dragons. I believe that how we use our imagination as children, affects us later in life.

We can not live our dreams through our children and we do them a great injustice when we push them into being over-achievers. They only have one child-hood. All too soon they will be adults and take on the responsibilities of being an employee a father/mother, husband/wife, bread-winner. Yes, we can steer them and encourage them, even use a little leverage because we know how important it is that they graduate from high school, but they still need time to be kids and enjoy their childhood.

Above all, we need to believe in our kids. We have planted the seeds when they were young and now we need to trust them. It is not easy to do in these times when there is so much trouble that kids can get into. And, not for a split second do I believe that because a kid does go off the rails, he was not loved and encouraged as a child. Parents sometimes go through excruciating guilt when this happens. Even in the same family, some kids survive and stay on a safe path and one kid may end up with a drug problem. I don't know the answer.

I pray a lot. I talk to the Lord a lot about my children. "Lord, I taught the kids when they were little. All I can do is trust you and them." Every day, I put them in His care. I've done my fair share of worrying and fretting. Today I have an affirmation for my children. "My children are blessed, happy and make good decisions about their lives."

As I said before, my son is twenty now and has his own apartment and car. He became independent without the help of his parents. He graduated when he was seventeen and was accepted into a university but, due to circumstances, was unable to go. He dropped out of the Junior College and continued to work and live in this small town. It made me sad to see him stay here and work so hard when most of his school friends were off at college. I had a really tough time with all of it.

I was finally able to let go of it. After all. He is a very together twenty year old, and I can trust him to make the right decision.

Yes, love never fails. And throw in there large quantities of faith and hope. My friend shared, "Sarah, most kids have two parents. I know that you love your kids. If you can, love them twice as much." Maybe that is why I loved them so much. I was loving them for two.

To say that being a single parent is a tough job is definitely an understatement, and there may be times that you feel that you can not do more than you are doing already. But I will still say to you as John once said to me, "Most kids have two parents. I know that you love your kids. If you can love them twice as much."

Chapter 6

A Time to Remember Precious Moments

As parents, we certainly experience some touching moments. Sometimes we hear such profound things come out of our childrens' mouths. We really could write a book on the things they say. We think we'll never forget but alas we do. Wish I had written them down. But not to worry, some of them are just written in my heart by now. They are safe there.

Suzanne still makes me laugh. All of a sudden she will remember something she used to believe when she was little. One day, when she was about 5 years old she laughed and said, "Mom, you know that when I was little and we were driving home at night, I used to think that God put the moon in the sky to show us the way home." How precious. In her little childhood eyes, He was our friend. He loved us so much, He gave us a special light at night to lead us home in the dark. It still makes me smile, from the depths of my heart, because it is true!

Noah, Suzanne and I were special. And we had a big shiny moon in the sky to prove it. Wish we could keep those childlike minds. We are special. God loves us. He puts a big light in the sky at night, like a great big light bulb.

And I hope I believe this till the day I die. Lord, Thank You for that big light in the sky. You put it there just for us, 'cuz you love Noah, Suzanne and I so much.

And I hope that my children believe it all of their lives. Many songs have been written about the moon. But this little child, so loved and secure, thought that it was God's flash-light just for us. P.S. I'm glad we had head lights for those windy roads in Ft. Bragg.

Noah's Christmas

It was just a few days before Christmas in wintry Ft. Bragg. I worked in a small country hospital and work had been canceled (due to low census). The kids and I were driving home and my heart was so sad because there was no money available to buy a present each for the kids. This really was a sad mom.

Noah was about six at the time. He was such a wise caring little character. Out of the blue, his sweet little voice said, "Mom, don't worry. Christmas is really Jesus' birthday. We don't need presents, we should be getting presents for Jesus."

Today even as I type, this memory brings tears to my eyes. And every Christmas, I ponder on the sweet little six year old who understood what Christmas was all about.

Christmas is a wonderful time of the year. It is a time of giving. We share a wonderful meal and most of us get to enjoy a family reunion.

Can you imagine how Christmas could really be if we gave presents to Jesus? How do we do that? He said that whatsoever we do to one of these my children, you do unto Me. Imagine, if we gave all that money (probably still on our credit cards) to the hungry children of the world? What a Christmas that would be!

Chapter
Suzanne's Baby

When Suzanne was little, she persisted that I have another baby. I explained to her many times that I could not. So eventually she stopped asking.

Then one day she said, "Mom how come pay day is over and you didn't get our baby?" I was stumped! Couldn't imagine what pay day had to do with a baby. In my mind the question went unanswered. Then one day she asked me if I would buy something for her. I said, "Sure honey but we have to wait until pay day". Then it dawned on me. This poor child was so used to her mom waiting until pay day, that when I said that I couldn't have a baby (and assumed she understood). She thought I meant, "Wait until pay-day."

Pay day never came to buy that little baby. That's O.K. Now she is looking forward to having her own babies in the future and I am looking forward to having grandchildren. Now she knows that it takes more than money and a grocery store. It takes time and a lot of love. Think she realizes too, that though most women can have a baby, not every woman can be the mother a baby needs.

I've tried to teach my children well, but that does not mean that they will not experience unwanted pregnancies. I pray they will not. We've talked about teenage pregnancy and how it can change a teenager's life. Don't be afraid to discuss this with your children. Babies are not dolls that we take out of the cupboard to play with.

Our sons also need to know that they will be held accountable. It takes two to make a baby. They need to know how life-changing an unplanned pregnancy can be.

No, we can't go to the grocery store and buy a baby Suzanne, and we can't return it and get our money back. It is yours to love forever no matter what!

Noah's Christmas
Part 2

Maybe it was the same Christmas, it's hard to tell. We had some rough ones. Once again we were out of funds. No tree, no turkey and no presents to put under the tree.

Little Noah was always coming up with ideas that he was excited about. One day he said, "Mom, if we were having presents, know what would be a neat idea? Wrap Suzanne's in one kind of Christmas wrap and mine in another kind. Wouldn't that be fun?" I still remember his enthusiasm, his excitement!

A few days before Christmas, a friend delivered a little Christmas tree. He didn't exactly steal it. After all, we were surrounded by thousands of acres of trees. These friends also gave us a turkey. Somehow they ended up having two turkeys. That same day, my mother arrived from Ireland and that, in itself, was a wonderful treat.

On the way back from the airport, my mother listened as Noah told his Christmas wrap idea with his usual exuberance. She just smiled at me and later whispered, "I have a suitcase full of presents from back home."

It was Christams Eve and when the kids went to sleep, I snuck out to the store. I bought two different kinds of Christmas wrap. What a Christmas Eve we had. My mom and I sat like two thieves in the night, wrapping presents in two kinds of wrapping paper.

Don't need to tell you the excitement on Christmas morning and they knew immediately which presents belonged to whom. They were happy wee bairns on Christmas morn.

And you know, I miss those Christmases. Not just because the kids are older, but because there is something about Christmas when we receive gifts of love. A little stolen tree which was never missed, a donated turkey, the sweetest mom in the world, presents hand delivered from a very special family in Ireland, and presents wrapped in two kinds of paper.

The fondest Christmas memories we share are from those Christmases when we had little and saw "love come down at Christmas."

A Mother's Love

MOM. "What's in a name? A rose by any other name would smell as sweet." It makes me think of the scene in Bambi, where he was learning words. They pointed out a flower and he said, "Flower." Then they introduced Bambi to a Skunk and he said, "Flower." What is in a name? Even more so now as an adult, the name "mom" conjures up some warm, loving feelings. Here is someone (a mom), who loves me deeply. My heart is with those who cannot share these feelings, because no matter how bad things were, no matter how rough life was, I knew that at least one person loved me very, very much. That person was "my wee mom."

When Suzanne was little, we used to have these play arguments. I would think of my mom and say, "Suzanne, I have the best mom in the whole world." She would respond, "No, I have the best mom in the whole world." I wish that we all had the best mom in the world. I believe that a mom loves a child even when no-one else does (this goes for dads also). A mom just loves and keeps on loving. A parent's love for a child is one of the greatest forces in the world.

Recently my son said to me, "Mom, why do you worry?" (After all, he is 19 now and does not need anyone to worry about him). I responded proudly, "Because I am your mother and it is my privilege to worry. Telling me not to worry is like telling the rain not to fall in Ireland." He laughed.

A child cannot even start to comprehend the concern and prayers of a parent's heart until he grows up and becomes a parent himself, so I didn't share my whole heart. I could have told him, "Not only do I have concern about you, but for the woman that you will choose to be your wife and the children that you will father."

As mothers you have probably struggled with this already. They cannot learn from our mistakes; they have to learn it all by themselves. We give them lots of love, teach them good, old fashioned principles, determine not to control and over protect them and we pray and keep our hands behind our backs when it is time to let go. Tough isn't it? Because we do love with a mother's heart.

We know that the decisions they make now might strongly, negatively or positively, affect their lives for decades or even for the rest of their lives. We know also, that no matter what they do, we will still love them. Yes, we will love and we will worry.

Is there a limit to a parent's love? I believe there is not. Sometimes that love is so painful because it does not have limits. It cannot be shut off and on. It can be strong and tough, but it never stops. Undoubtedly there are many of you who could write incredible stories about loving children through, and in spite of, mistakes and consequences.

My mother could write such a story. I have told you my side of the story, how she loved me in spite of all my mistakes. She was there, ready to pick up the pieces. She raised me well but I had to do it my way. Nonetheless, she was there and she still believes in me. She didn't discard me or write me off. No, she is still a wonderful friend. Perhaps my best friend, six thousand miles away.

What amazes me is how perceptive she is. She is so funny. Many years ago, she learned that when I do not call home, it usually means that life isn't going too well. This makes me smile because it is true, the reason being obvious, I suppose. I didn't want to burden her when I hit a rough spot, because I knew that she would worry. When life was a little easier I would call and share good things. I did not realize that I was doing this but she caught on very fast.

I could not fool my mother. Mothers know. How do mothers know? I don't know. Believing what I personally believe, I would claim that this gift is God given. I'm not talking here about mothers who control their children and who have not learned to let go. That is a problem and a whole other subject. I am writing here about a mother's innate ability to know when all is not right in her child's life.

My mom has often said, "Sarah, you can't hide it from me. I just know because I feel it in my heart. But it's O.K. I just pray." And pray she does. Don't ignore those tugs in your heart. Pray and keep praying. You may not believe as I believe but there probably isn't one of us who hasn't cried out in our hour of need. When you feel that burden, don't be afraid to cry out. Those words will not go unheard. Who better to watch over your child that the One who created him/her. Don't be too proud to ask for help. Do it for the sake of your children.

I've heard "faith" defined as "something believed in, not yet seen." I personally could not have raised my children alone without faith or prayer. Just this morning, I had this sudden heaviness in my heart for one of my children. He is a very together nineteen year old and I am pleased about having such a wonderful son. My heart hurt for him and I did not even know why. So, I got on my knees and ended up crying. I cried and cried. My heart was so burdened. I had spoken to him just a few days before and he was O.K.

I had left a message on his dad's answering machine and he returned my call. Something unpleasant was happening in his life. I told him what had happened and he said, "Mom, how did you know that I felt bad?" Yes, we hurt when they hurt. Are there words to describe a parent's love? I believe, "probably not."

Now I know just a little of what my mother experienced. Wow, what a lot to put her through. Mom, Thank you for loving me in spite of myself and thank you for being there. I believe with all my heart that there is no love on earth like a mother's love. I thank the Lord for choosing you to be my mother.

P.S. Mom, do me a favor. Pray that my kids don't put me through what I put you through. Pray hard!!!

The Gas Station Attendant

I worked every other weekend, so every other Sunday, the kids and myself went to church. Friends helped me out a lot with child care, so often on Sunday, I would repay the favor and take other kids after church. Sometimes they played around Happy Acre and sometimes I would take them to the beach.

One Sunday, after church, I stopped to get gas. I had six kids with me, I believe, and they were a happy bunch. The gas attendant's name was embroidered on his shirt. Noah, being his usual exuberant, happy self, said, "Hey Bob, how ya doin'?" The gas attendant obviously liked kids, he said, "I'm fine. What's your name?" And, of course, he said, "Noah." Then Bob said to the next kid, "And what's your name?" He said, "Nathan." Bob looked surprised and said to another boy, "And what's your name?" He said, "Isaiah." Now Bob really looked surprised.

Bob had finished pumping gas, etc. and looking through the back window, said to Suzanne, "And I suppose your name is Sarah." I was starting the car and said to him, "No, but mine is." We all thought this scenario funny and had a good laugh. Bob watched as we drove away. If he had only known that the names of the remaining two kids were Sharon and Matthew. Many a time I remember the gas station attendant's face and have a chuckle to myself.

Our Garden, Where the Purdies Grow

There's a very old song that says, "I'll meet you in the garden, where the Purdies grow." I am assuming that it is an old Irish song, because Ireland might be the only country where they talk about Purdies. Purdies are known to be the staple of the Irish diet and for those of you who do not know, Purdies are plain ol' potatoes and are very much a part of Irish history.

In fact, it was the potato or, I should say, the blight of the potato, that explains the number of Irish folks living in these good old United States. Potatoes grow well in Ireland, due to the climate. They were a great part of the Irish diet. When the "Blight" hit the potatoes in Ireland, it is true, millions of people died of hunger and starvation. There was famine and those with the strength or resources fled to the shores of America.

Thousands of those who boarded ship, to challenge the crossing of the cold Atlantic, never made it to these shores, the great big country known as the land of "milk and honey". The blight was finally wiped out and in the meantime, the Wild Irish established themselves. I love Irish history and a short paragraph does a great injustice to those who dared to cross the Atlantic so many years ago.

Back then, this was a fierce country and not the country we know today. It is so easy to forget that. Apparently, potatoes grew here. They were cultivated by the Native Americans. I'm sure the Irish Immigrants were happy to see their beloved potato and planted many more.

We Irish love our Purdies and I wanted to grow our own. This was just the right place to grow them and right by my side was the wee Irish mom who knew how.

About three weeks after we arrived in our new town, a new friend at work told me about a place for rent out in the woods. It was three miles inland and far from neighbors. To this day I cannot imagine why the description of the place was so unappealing to me. For some reason it produced a reaction of fear. I think I had seen too many movies. I did not want to go see the place but in the course of conversation, mentioned it to my mother who immediately wanted to drive out into the country to see it.

I don't know why I was reluctant to see the place, because I was used to living in the country. It had something to do with being alone with two little children, out in the trees, miles away from civilization. Anyway, we set off to look for the place in the woods. We were totally lost. However, after driving around for what seemed like a long time, we happened to see a lady who was walking to her car. We described the place and asked if she could possibly direct us to the property.

I was fairly taken aback when the lady said, "Why yes, that is the property that I am renting out". It was quite a coincidence considering that we were in the boonies. She offered to show the property to us. We were so happy that we had bumped into her.

I fell in love at first sight. It was the most wonderful place in the world to me. This was the little home in the country that I had dreamed of for so many years and beside the ocean, too. What a wonderful gift.

The woods consisted of pine and redwood trees. The double-wide trailer had two bedrooms, an adorable kitchen, a covered porch and a car port. In it was a large wood-burning stove. The acre was sunny because it was three miles from the ocean and consequently from the fog. There was so much open space and so many trees to climb.

At the beginning of the driveway was a fenced in area for a garden. It was huge and already fenced off from the deer. All I could think of was planting a garden in the spring. We could grow lots of vegetables and even grow our own potatoes. What a happy day it was when we found our little happy acre out in the woods!

As I've mentioned before, those first months were tough financially but we loved all the wonderful things about our happy little home. We went for walks and explored the area. We enjoyed that big wood burning stove and spent many happy hours in front of it. Spring was a treat. Wild flowers popped up all over the place and the birds sang their little hearts out. There was life everywhere.

Finally, it was time to start digging. We dug square beds and oblong beds and then, of course, we dug drills for the Purdies. I was working evening shift, which means that I worked from three P.M. until eleven-thirty P.M. That meant, of course, that I had the morning at home with the kids and my mother who stayed much longer than she had planned on staying. The kids were too young to go to school, so all four of us were together and working in the garden.

That was a wonderful time in my life. The sun shone, the birds sang and I was out in the garden with my three most favorite people in the whole world. We ate lunches outside in the sunshine. For a treat, my mother would make bread on the griddle. What a happy bunch we were.

We spent so many wonderful hours in our garden. We worked like beavers. One morning, I said to my mom, "Mom, do you think I will ever in my life be able to have a place like this? I love it so much." My mom is a tiny little person but her faith is not tiny by any means. She leaned on her spade and said, "Sarah, I believe that one day, the Lord will give this place to you." I just looked back at her. She really did have amazing faith; but I didn't have a penny. I had lost everything.

The garden grew and so did the occupants who lived on that happy acre. We had vegetables to give away. It was a wonderful summer just as it had been a wonderful spring. In the fall my mother returned to Ireland. Our lives changed once more and we had to adapt to new things. A babysitter who wasn't Grandma, daycare bills, making dinner after work. I know that the kids missed Grandma's walks, Grandma's bedtime stories and especially Grandma's Irish soda bread but by then we were stronger and more settled. I ate the purdies and thought of her very often, knowing that she was enjoying her purdies with her other daughters back home. I didn't think much about what she shared with me in the garden. I did continue to love and enjoy our Happy acre and dreamed occasionally of being settled there. About a year later, my mother did return and we were so happy to see her again. She stayed long enough to plant another garden. That wonderful lady also showed up in California with a down payment on "Happy Acre" which was now for sale.

I cannot even start to tell you how special that was. You see, my mother had sold her own home to come up with the money. We enjoyed many "precious moments" there. My brother visited and he and the kids built a tree house. We added a third bedroom (with the help of wonderful friends) and we built the deck that my mother often dreamed of. The happy acre grew. We had not only our garden but chickens, kitties and a dog. We even had a "Happy Acre Day-care Center."

When the subject of gardening comes up in conversation, my thoughts wander to the garden at Happy Acre, my very special mother, all those wonderful memories and the Purdies that we grew so long ago.

She Wasn't Kidding

When I finally and reluctantly left my marriage, I moved to a small fishing, logging town on the coast. It was a pretty scary move but a move that was much needed. I had borrowed money from my sister in Ireland for the first month's rent and the fee for a U-Haul. To say that the move was scary is an understatement. Yes, it was good to be turning a page and starting a new chapter in my life but it was awesome.

The rent was paid for the first month, now it was up to me to find work and provide for this little family. It was a happy day when I started work at the local hospital. As it turned out, there were four of us who started work that day and what a great group my new friends were. All four of us had names that started with S's or C's. All four of us were very different but became very close.

C was hilarious and kept us laughing with her shameless humor. Her husband had grown up in our little town and they had moved from Los Angeles to raise their kids close to their grand-parents. She was a riot. She and her husband became close friends. The other C was quite newly wed and was more reserved. She and her husband had left Southern California to start a life in the country. Both couples were building a home in the woods. They also became very close friends. S was single, lived a traveling life similar to my own and moved to our small fishing town to be with her boy-friend. We were a real mix. All new to the area and all new on the job.

Hilarious C taught us much about the area and told us lots of funny stories. She kept us in laughs all day long. One day, we were talking about slugs, simply because it was impressive, the number of slugs all over the place. The kids loved this of course, because for some strange reason, kids love slugs. UGH!!! C really got off on a roll and told us about these slugs that are extremely slimy and were black and yellow. She told us they were about ten to twelve inches long and were called Banana slugs. Yuck, what a thought! A slug that looked like a banana and was just as big as a banana. Well, of course, I knew she was pulling my leg. There couldn't be such an ugly creature. She involved other locals in her attempt to convince me but there was no way I was falling for such a tale. I wasn't a city girl, like the others. I grew up in Ireland and there was no slug on earth as big as a banana.

Soon after this huge snail tale, our little troop moved out of town to Happy Acre. This was country living. It wasn't country living from a magazine, it was the real thing and we loved it. Life, far from the "maddening crowd." The real McCoy. It isn't long before you see your first banana slug when you live in dem dar woods and I have to tell you, I was horrified. I'm not a wimp when it comes to living in the woods but I really was grossed out. C had not exaggerated one bit. Yes, they were huge and yes, they were black and yellow. UGH!!! What C failed to tell us was that there were hundreds of them. They were all over the place.

I love to camp and when it was warm enough, we had our first camping trip to the Navarro River. It was a great spot. Redwood trees and a sandy beach going down to the river. I had camped there with my husband and we had a great time. The river was perfect for swimming and canoeing. That was before I knew about Banana slugs. Yes, they were there. Before, I did not know they existed. Now, I saw them with my own eyes. We slept in the woods, under the stars as was the custom. I lay awake, listening to the quiet, sleeping snores around me but I was on guard all night long. I kept watch all night long to ward off the attack of the Banana slugs. During my travels, I had many escapades but sharing my sleeping bag with multitudes of Banana slugs was a nightmare. It was a long night.

Over the years I learned to live with the Banana slug population. They were on the outside and I was on the inside. They multiplied in the winter. In the mornings, they were over the windows and all over the deck. They were just there and that was life in the country. I pulled the curtains and walked carefully on the deck when I left for work in the mornings. Banana slugs loved our Happy Acre and I learned to not look and to not stand on them. Oh, the joys of country living.

One night I went home from work after working the P.M. shift. The kids were away at their Dad's, and I busied around trying to keep warm. I took the garbage outside to the garbage can. It was dark in the car-port but I knew my way around. I put my hand on the lid to remove it and YES, it was disgusting. Even tonight, it grosses me out big time. I ran inside and washed my hands. I washed and washed and still the slime would not wash off. I had done the dreaded thing. I cannot even say what I did but you know already. After learning to live with them and avoid them, I had finally shaken hands with one of those little critters.

The moral of the story is; do not empty the trash in the dark, because you do not know what monsters lurk in the dark. I now believe in Banana slugs because they are real, but never shake hands with one. It is only the advice of a wimp but you will regret it very, very much. And you will remember the encounter for a long, long time. Buy an over the counter lubricant. It will wash off a lot easier.

P.S. I hope I don't dream about Banana slugs. They are slimy, I'm sure, even in dreams.

Red, Yellow, Black and White

When my kids were young, there was so much that I did not know. There were so many good things to learn. Actually, so much of what I was learning, I should have known already, and I don't know why I did not already know these things.

Maybe it was because I did not have my first child until I was twenty-six, and had not experienced the responsibility of owning a home until I was in my thirties. Maybe I had just spent too much time on the road, living in different countries. I do not know the answer. What I do know, is that when the time came, I wanted to learn and grow. I started to read. There was not much time to read back then, but as the years went on and the market became swamped with self-help books, I was there grabbing them up. They may not be every body's cup of tea, but I know that I personally benefited from them. Actually, I drove my co-workers crazy.

I knew about having dreams, and had actually had several dreams come true before I was twenty-four years old. I didn't know though about setting goals, so together, the kids and myself learned how to set and write goals. What fun we had. Little Peanut drew lines and wrote some letters. Noah really got into this. He'd rest his little chin in cupped hands, elbows on the table. Then he would smile and write something.

We took this stuff seriously and wrote on our four by six recipe cards. Peanut continued to draw her goals, working her way through the stack of recipe cards and Noah made a list resembling a list for Santa Claus. Short term goals were easier for Noah, and my heart is still so touched when I come across his recipe card. In the uneven printing of a very funny five year old, is written, "Milk and cookies." Yes, these were the short term goals of the Cookie Monster.

Writing goals was a good experience and I still do this, simply because if I write the goal, I am also obligated to write down some steps and actions I need to take to reach the goal. Sometimes I come across the goals that I wrote back then. Most were realistic, some were not and that is O.K., too. Anyway, there is still time, I hope.

Besides sailing around the world (hey, life begins at forty), my biggest dream was to adopt many children. Somehow I was going to raise a lot of money and buy a house large enough for lots of little kids to live in. The kids and myself used to sit around and talk about it. We needed a huge kitchen table and a back yard big enough for a baseball field. We would need a couple of vans and more than one driver.

The children who lived with us would be every color and nationality. Red, yellow, black and white. Irish, Japanese, Korean, Mexican, African, Indian. I would just love them all so much and we would be so happy together. What wonderful Christmases we would have! How well loved those kids would be. How great their self-esteem would be, growing up with so much love.

This is one of the dreams which did not come true for me. I love kids so much and they still steal my heart away. Once, as I traveled across

North Africa, our little group sat down by the side of the road (I might venture to call it a road) and ate a lunch of bread and oranges.

As we sat and ate, we were joined by a curious little kid. He was so beautiful. He was about six years old and looked so healthy. The whites of his eyes were huge and stark against his dark shiny skin. He was quiet and timid. With time he was joined by other little fellows around the same age. They stared and did not say anything. Perhaps, we were the only white people they had ever seen. How strange we must have looked to them with our pale anemic looking skin and tattered blue jeans.

I made several attempts to talk to them in French, which was the language they spoke, but they were very shy and did not respond. Besides, the Parisian French that I spoke with an Irish accent was far removed from the language they were accustomed to hearing. I took my guitar and sang old Sunday school choruses that I had learned as a child, but they did not recognize these songs. However, they appeared to enjoy the music. They continued to stare and would smile at each other, but they never spoke.

I will never forget those happy, beautiful faces. They were so innocent and free of pain. I remember this scene as if it happened just yesterday. I sang for quite a long time and they listened so politely.

According to the map, this was a "B" class road. In actual fact, the road did not exist. A bridge had collapsed and consequently, there was no traffic on the road. We hiked many miles along that road in the hot blazing sun. Shortly after this incident, I became ill with septicemia and I will spare the details of how that came to be.

My body was covered with red raised welts, I literally could not eat for weeks and I was so weak. I was carrying a back-pack and a guitar. The sun was ruthless and the road without cars was endless. We walked and walked for what seemed to me a long time, days in fact. As I trudged along, putting one foot in front of the other, I had wonderful memories of those beautiful children, so happy and content in their world, even though they had so little. I did finally recover, very many pounds lighter and malnourished but I never did forget those little kids with their very dark brown skin and huge velvet brown eyes, so kind and full of love.

Several years later, I was going to Mexico, from California with my husband at the time. He had traveled to Mexico before and knew the need of many who lived there. Before our trip, he went to yard sales and bought lots of kid's clothes to give to the kids that we would meet. Again, I remember the love and appreciation on those darling little faces as they lit up in surprise when he gave the clothes to them. Those beautiful big brown eyes that danced for joy. These kids had so little, yet they were so happy.

We lived in a very small fishing village there, right on the ocean. The villagers accepted us into their lives. They only fished three days a week because the catch was sufficient to feed their families and usually they shared their catch with us. The women were a little shy at first, but as I went daily to the river to wash clothes, they finally learned to trust me. What I remember most though, are the two children that visited so frequently throughout the day. Little Toribio was about two years old and had a perpetual smile from ear to ear. He was shy, but still came to visit often. Korina was nine years old, a little lady and a very pretty one. She visited often and taught us how to make refried beans. They are in their twenties and thirties now. I think of them from time to time and wonder how they are doing.

Then of course, there were the adorable children in Greece who went out with their parents on special occasions and loved to dance. I loved the Greek Festivals because everybody danced, even the tiniest of children. How did they learn to dance like that?

And I cannot forget those little kids in Canada, who, it seemed to me, learned to skate on the ice before they even learned to walk. They were amazing.

Undoubtedly, I was the only one on the rink who did not know how to skate and resembled a baby elephant wearing ice skates for the first time. I would be making panicked maneuvers to reach the rail of the rink, legs involuntarily further apart by the second, and these energetic little toddlers would be skating under my legs and laughing. They thought it was so funny. I thought they were wonderful.

It is no wonder to me that I wanted kids of my own, and no wonder at all that I wanted to adopt little kids of every color and nationality. Kids are so special. It is unfortunate, but true, that their childhood so often determines the adult they will become. What a wonderful world we would live in if every child was loved and grew to love himself, knowing that the world was a great place to live, and that his or her contribution was respected and appreciated.

My dream of adopting children, Red, Yellow, Black, and White, did not come to pass, but my heart is still with each and every one. My heart is with the kids in the ghettos who have no dreams, they have grown up there and they know from what they have seen that there is no hope. They have no dreams of going to college or doing something wonderful with their lives. It tears at my heart and makes it ache. For so many, there is no hope. Yes, it is true, in a country as affluent as ours, for some, there is no hope. So often we turn a blind eye to the violence in our society. We are quick to judge those who are less fortunate. How can we judge until we have walked in their moccasins. We cannot even start to imagine life without hope.

There are children with wonderful minds, who want to learn and move ahead, but will never have an opportunity to do so. Instead they become victims of the society to which they could have contributed much. We can never know the pain and the grief that they experience in life.

Martin Luther had a dream; I have the same dream and I hope you do also. All the little children, Red, Yellow, Black and White, all are precious in His sight. All should have the same opportunity, but in reality they do not. My dream was to take just a handful and give them hope and an opportunity that they might not have had before.

As I raised my kids alone and worked hard, I had an idyllic dream that was close to my heart. I would work hard and stay committed to the task at hand and one day I would live by the ocean, have a garden, knit till my heart was content and write books. That dream is more real now than it ever was. It is still a far out there dream, but more feasible than ever before. I still want that dream to come true, but I know in my heart that it would not make me happy. Why do I say this? Because I know that I could not just kick back and enjoy this wonderful life style knowing that there was so much need around me in this world.

Somehow, somewhere, I will need to know that my life here on earth is contributing to those in need. I cannot hide myself away in my idyllic world and close my eyes to the grief and pain around me. I could never hoard money, knowing that it could be used to bless another. My family and some friends support an orphanage in India. I had a dream that one day I would be able to buy land for them in India and build a new home for them.

As it was, it was tough financially to raise two kids alone and I did not have money to send my own son to college even though he was an honor student. Yes, a mind is a terrible thing to waste, Red, Yellow, Black or White. All over the world, there are kids going without (we need to remember this when we look at our own situation). I have not given up hope. Maybe I will live in a little secluded cottage by the ocean one day.

Maybe I will join the Peace Corps and help many beautiful little children after I have raised my own. In the meantime, I will love my own children and reach out to those around me. I have single parent friends who are very busy. I will offer to take their children to the ocean or other fun places. Right now I have a busy schedule and cannot adopt children. In the meantime I will reach out to the kids I do know and try to bless them in any way possible. Martin Luther had a dream which I wish every American strived to make a reality in this country.

I am a dreamer. Sometimes I think to myself, what if Martin Luther's dream was to become the battle cry of these United States. Children of today are the leaders of tomorrow. The future of this world seems dismal; many of those children are sorely disadvantaged. My dream is that every child would have the opportunity to reach his/her full potential, Red, Yellow, Black or White.

Our First Funeral

We had planned on leaving Happy Acre and moving back to the town where the children's father lived. However, our plans were delayed for a year and we rented a house in town. It was a great old house and, except for wanting the children to be close to their father and needing to be in an area where there was more work, we would have been very happy to live in this house for a long time.

The whole upstairs was an attic. The attic was huge, with two bedrooms and a bathroom. It even had a balcony and French windows. I created a den up there with a couch and TV. There were two walk-in closets, each big enough to be bedrooms. Of course, Suzanne turned one of them into a bedroom for her babies. It was a great house to live in and we enjoyed it a lot.

It was in this house that Suzanne finally got the hamster she had wanted for so long. She and the hamster spent many happy hours in the attic with her babies. He was a pleasant little feller and she gave him lots of lovin'. He was her best buddy.

One evening at work, I received a distressed call from the babysitter who was at my house with the kids. Hermie had died and Suzanne was so upset. I tried to talk to her on the phone, but could not appease her. She was heart broken. I went home on my dinner break and she was doing those little involuntary sobbings that just break a mother's heart. I told her that we would buy another hamster but she grieved for Hermie. He had been her little friend.

Next morning, we had a funeral for Hermie and buried him in the backyard. She made her final farewell to her little friend.

We did buy another hamster and he was a lively one. While we had him, we moved to this town where we rented a little house. He was wilder than Hermie. Once he escaped and we could not find him. He was missing for days and we were afraid that he had run away from home. We were starting to give up hope.

One day, I was rummaging around in the bottom of my closet and was horrified at what I discovered. The rug was all chewed up. I mean, it was really chewed up and not just a little. I sat and stared at the damage. Out of the corner of my eye I spied a lonely little hamster. It was a happy reunion but the land lady charged an arm and half of a leg for the damages when we left there. At least we did not need to have a funeral for a hamster that was no longer with us.

Not too long after this, we were house sitting for my friend. Now, this was an absolutely beautiful house with off white thick carpet throughout. We took Freddie with us, of course, we couldn't leave little Freddie behind. Well, we were having a good time there. There were decks everywhere, a custom pool with some palm trees around it and a wonderful view of the valley. The house had a pool room with ferns and white wicker furniture. It was a nice vacation.

Yes, we were having a great vacation until one day, Suzanne came to me with an alarmed look on her face and said, "Mom, Skippy is gone." I freaked. Skippy loose in a house that was almost four thousand square feet. And all that carpet. I was a basket case. We looked high and we looked low. We looked inside and we looked outside. I thought of Skippy in a closet having a feast of carpet, and I thought of Skippy being eaten by the dog. We looked for that little critter till I was seeing hamsters in my sleep.

The worst part was telling my friends when they returned from their trip. Yes, the dogs were fine, but there was a "moose loose a boot this hoose." (there was a mouse loose about this house). The story has an O.K. ending. My friend never did find Skippy and there was no damage to report. Suzanne did not grieve the same for him, even though she mentioned him sometimes and wondered what on earth could have happened to him?

I guess she was just growing up and learning to deal with life better. She still talks often about getting a pet again. I shudder when she mentions hamsters. Worse still, she talks about wanting a chameleon. Now, that really makes me shudder. Being from Ireland, I didn't grow up with lizards and other reptiles, so I don't find them as adorable as Suzanne does. I have these awful images of them escaping and crawling over the bed. Ugh!!! And, snakes are out of the question.

She wants a dog for Christmas and I would love one also. Now, dogs don't eat rugs, but they sure play havoc in the garden. Personally, I would love to have my own horse again but I don't think the neighbors or "the City" would approve. It's time to move out into the country soon, where we will be able to have dogs, horses, chickens and lots of little animals. All of the above, but no hamsters, snakes or reptiles, thank you.

Suzanne's Goldfish

Suzanne loved animals and she was always asking for pets. One night we went to a carnival at her school. It turned out to be a very special night for her because she won goldfish in a plastic bag. What a happy kid she was her very own goldfish.

We were all very tired when we got home, but being mom, I found a bowl suitable for her darling little fish. She was elated. Her very own tiny little fish to care for. It was late and we wanted to go to bed, but she was as hyper as a kid could be. All of a sudden she asked a very appropriate question. "Mom, what will my goldfish eat?" I was scurrying around trying to get things together for the "morning Exodus".

I guess it was a typical scene with mom buzzing around, trying to do forty, things at once, and at the same time trying to deal with real problems like "What will the goldfish eat?" I came into the living room to find my creative little daughter crumbling crackers into the fish bowl.

"What a great idea!" I thought, which just goes to show how on the ball I was.

In spite of a couple of comments from mom that it was time to go to bed, Suzanne continued to view the fish bowl with fascination and contentment. Suddenly I heard distressed cry, "Mom, something is wrong with my fishie". I ran to the scene and sure enough the goldfish were in distress." Something was very wrong. Now, I was used to dealing with respiratory distress with humans, but I didn't have a clue what to do for these little fish.

Suzanne was in even worse distress than the fish were. She cried and could not be appeased. I reassured her that I would buy more fish for her, but to no avail. She was devastated and there was nothing that I could do to appease her. You've heard me say before, "The crazy things we do for our kids." Well, this was the craziest. I didn't know how to do CPR on a fish, but before I knew what I was doing, I was blowing tiny little breaths for that little fishie (I'm embarrassed to admit this).

That little fish did not survive my CPR and I had a broken hearted little girl. It did dawn on me why the fish died. You've probably guessed already, right? It was the salty crackers. We killed the fish with kindness.

P.S. The fish did not survive but Suzanne did.

Goodbye Rotten Old Appendix

My son was very stoic and usually did not complain when he did not feel well. One day though, he did complain of abdominal pain. Being a nurse I did a thorough check for appendicitis. The pain went away and it was all forgotten about. The following evening he complained again of abdominal pain. He said that the pain was there all day, but he just ignored it. His temperature was one hundred and two.

I called the doctor, of course. We both agreed that it probably wasn't appendicitis, because the fever usually wasn't as high with appendicitis, but that I should wait and see what happened. I drove into town and bought some medicine for his fever. In the morning, when I woke up, he was lying on the floor, beside my bed. I felt so bad. He said, "If I lie with my legs bent up, it doesn't hurt as bad."

Off we went to the doctor's office. By one o'clock that afternoon, he was in surgery having his appendix removed. I should say, having his ruptured appendix removed. I felt so bad that I did not know he had been hurting so long.

By nine o'clock that evening he was out of bed and walked to the bathroom. He was a little trooper. Within a couple of days though, he started to vomit and his abdomen was distended. He had what was called an Ileus, quite typical after a ruptured appendix. This meant that he had to have a naso-gastric tube passed through his nose, into his stomach and the tube would then be attached to suction to drain away the fluid.

Having a naso-gastric tube passed is a very unpleasant experience as some of you may well know. Once, when I was a student nurse back in Ireland, we had to practice passing naso-gastric tubes. I was the guinea pig that day and I'm here to tell you that it was a terrible experience. I have a healthy appetite, but my appetite said goodbye for a while.

Noah was only nine but he was a model patient. There he sat in his chair with his I.V. and tube in his nose. I got to see him often because he was in the area where I worked. My fellow nurses loved him and brought presents to him (he counted eleven). He was into transformers and he got lots of them. Not a bad trade - lose your appendix, which were rotten anyway, and go home with new toys.

After a week, he was discharged, minus the I.V. and tube. It was a happy day and he was starving .....that I.V. just didn't hit the spot. He was bored at home and anxious to be back at school. In fact, he begged to go back to school. So, after two long weeks, back to school he went, well advised not to over exert himself.

That rotten old appendix was never missed and we never looked back. He made a speedy recovery and in no time, life was back to normal. As parents we tend to over-react perhaps when kids complain of abdominal pain, but abdominal pain does warrant monitoring. When my son first complained of abdominal pain, I checked him for appendicitis. Rebound tenderness is typical of appendicitis but my son did not have rebound tenderness.

When I took him to the doctor's office, he did not have typical appendicitis pain but his pediatrician was a good doctor (I had worked with him for years) and he ordered Lab work. When there is an infection going on in our bodies, the white cell count is usually elevated. This is because the white cells are what fight infection in our bodies, and they increase in number to fight the infection. My son's white count was thirty thousand, which indicated that there was an infection going on.

The surgeon was called. This Surgeon was one of my favorite people and I was happy that he was called. He was a wonderful surgeon, and his bed-side manner should be taught at every Medical school in the country. He said, "The appendix needs to come out."

Yes, as parents we do tend to over-react to abdominal pain, but be aware of abdominal pain that persists. I am a nurse and I missed this one. Be familiar with childhood diseases. Don't be in the dark. My son's high fever threw us off but his fever was high because his appendix had already ruptured.

Know CPR

One day, I was waiting in the Pediatrician's office with the kids reading and waiting for our turn to see the doctor. Suddenly the door burst open and a young girl ran into the waiting room yelling, "His heart stopped, his heart stopped." She was carrying a baby and ran straight back toward the examination rooms. It was an awful site to see the terror on that young mother's face - I can still see it when I think about that day.

At work at the hospital the next day, I heard the story about the mom and baby. The baby's heart did indeed stop. The mother (whom I saw for myself was very young) started C.P.R. Not only did she do C.P.R. at home, but she drove and did C.P.R. at the same time. The baby lived. This young mother had saved her baby's life.

If the mother had not known how to do C.P.R., the baby probably would not have survived. Do you know how to do C.P.R.? It is not difficult to learn and it is a matter of life and death.

If you don't know how to do C.P.R., find out where you can be certified. Call the American Heart Association or Red Cross. If you take your child to a baby-sitter, check to see if she knows how to do C.P.R. My daughter took a class at the Elementary school so that she could baby-sit. Most high-school kids know how to do C.P.R. In fact, today, it seems like most people know how to do C.P.R.

Actually, it's pretty amazing how much kids today know. Many kids are responsible for saving lives, because they dialed 911 in an emergency. Check that your kids know what to do if a crisis should arise. Make sure that they know their address so that they can report an emergency. Better to be safe than sorry.

Chapter 7

A Time to Weep, A Time to Mourn

I believe I can truthfully say that writing this book has been one of the most enjoyable things that I have ever done in my whole life. This book may never be published, but even if it is not, writing it has been a great experience. I have shed many tears in front of this word-processor as I poured out my heart.

So often, when my children were little, I longed to write, but there was so little time to indulge in such a luxury. My days were full and there was so little time to do anything but raise the kids. Many times when I was in a jungle of confusion or feeling like I was drowning, I thought to myself, "One day I will write a book about being a single mother."

My life today, in many ways, is more stressful than before because of the work I do. I am on call twenty-four hours a day, seven days a week. Usually I work ten, twelve, fourteen hours a day, even though I am paid for eight hours of work. In July, I left such a job and worked out of town to do some consulting. I will not get into the details, but I ended up with two weeks off with pay, or so I thought (the money did not materialize).

Because I thought I was being paid, I felt very comfortable with my time off and actually relaxed a little. One evening as I sat in my back yard, I thought about the book that I had wanted to write for so long to encourage single moms. All of a sudden, the book just formatted in my head. It was incredible. All of my thoughts over those busy years came together and that evening, I started to write. My writing skills were not good, but what was in my heart poured out faster than I could write.

Job opportunities closed to me, even though I was well qualified. I did not question any of it. Somehow this felt right to me. I kept writing and miraculously, the money just seemed to be there to live on. It just felt like a wonderful gift to me, that after all my hard work over the years, I was given this time to realize yet another dream and write the book that I had thought of for so many years.

Doors continued to close for me, but I continued to write and not be discouraged. Finally there came a time after a couple of months when I really needed to go back to work. Finances were tight and a friend called and asked me to come work with her. I had wanted to change direction and go back to school, but learned that there really are not grants available to women in their forties.

I was nervous about going back to the same type of work because I felt that after doing this work and driving two hours a day, all creativity would be gone and I would never be able to write again. I'm happy to say that this proved to be not true and that I still had time to write. I thoroughly enjoyed those months of not working full-time, going to the coffee shop and writing during the day.

It was actually a great experience. I worked out of town three times and actually went to the East coast to work. I made money, but did not have a huge commitment to a job that absorbed my whole life. It really was a great three months and I hope that I have many more just like them.

Even though I have enjoyed writing and have been forced to look at many things in my life since I started to do so, I did realize something over the last few weeks. I noticed that some of the first things that I had jotted down as thoughts came to me, were the things that remained on the list and not written about. One of the remaining, unwritten about "things" was "The Hard Times." For some reason, I was procrastinating writing about the hard times. Yet, aren't the hard times a lot of what this book is all about.

So, I sit here on a Friday night with lots of time to write and unwillingly write about the things that were so much a part of my life as a single mother. The hard times are ever with us, but I guess that as we become stronger and learn to take life as it comes, we often do not see them as such. Life is what's happening while we are making plans. John Lennon said this before he was assassinated. Life can be rough, but as we grow older we learn to roll with the punches. When we are older, we learn that "this too will pass."

The rough times are rougher when we are younger. We are like reeds blowing in the wind. We do not know that we will survive and that this too will pass. We are in the midst of it and the blizzard is blowing. The wind howls around us and we are blown off track. We do not know from what has gone before. We are in the midst of a gale and it is relentless.

Perhaps the rough times for me were very rough because I had so much growing to do. I had so much to learn. Now I am kinder to myself and try to accept myself for who and what I am. I am just a sojourner on this earth, and as I travel through life, I will make many mistakes, and from these mistakes I will learn and grow. Sometimes learning is painful but only because I allow it to be so. I judge myself more harshly than my friends judge me.

Life was hard back then and I was a mess; everything was such a struggle. I was six thousand miles from home and raising two children alone. Being newly divorced, I was still dealing with a broken relationship and all the conflict that goes along with divorce. The anger and disillusionment on both sides. The disappointment of in-laws on both sides. All so preoccupied with their own pain that there is not much thought for the other party. It is so true, when divorce occurs, each person is so caught up in his own feelings that there is not much compassion left for what is happening in real life.

When I left, I was not aware of any emotional pain, because I was too busy trying to survive. I realize now that there had to be some emotional trauma. How can we make the commitment of marriage and leave without disappointment, regardless of the reason for a divorce? How can we be normal and together after such an experience? I did not face that reality in my life. I was just glad to have the opportunity to start over and be with my children in an environment free of friction. The truth is, (and I did not know it back then) it was devastating. I kid you not when I say that I was a mess.

I had left a marriage that was devastating and my self-esteem was rock-bottom. If my self-esteem had been intact, perhaps raising kids alone would have been easier. The problem is that most of us face this challenge after a divorce and whether we want to admit it or not, we have been through the mill. If this was not the case, we would probably still be married and we would not be single parents. With this alone, we are not off to a good start. Already we are weakened and do not know whether we are coming or going.

I was so caught up in what was happening that I certainly did not have the time or patience to deal with any of this. I dug in my heels and did what I had to do. I guess the finances were the toughest part to deal with. We were so broke. When I arrived at our destination, I had eighty dollars and an old car that leaked oil so badly, I had to put oil in it every time I put gas in it.

Stress undoubtedly effects our health, so mine was certainly not good. I was underweight and struggling with low blood-sugars. I described to my mother what happened if I went without food. I had learned not to leave home without Peanuts or another protein snack. One day, we walked into town (we lived in town then) and I felt my blood-sugar drop. I knew that I was heading for trouble and needed to eat. My mother did not understand and thought that I just wanted to eat. It used to happen so suddenly and it was quite new to me, but I knew that I needed to do something fast. It was too late and my mother saw how someone reacts to having a low blood-sugar. My mother raised me and knew that this was not how I usually behaved. She was shocked and I was a wreck. After that incident, she helped me and soon learned the signs of low blood sugars. Sometimes it happened so fast, I could not even help myself.

Friends at work helped also. I would break out into a cold sweat, but before that happened, I would be scattered and not able to think well. They would bring orange juice. One morning I remember just standing there, staring. I was sweating and my heart was raising. My lips were numb and I knew that I was going out fast. I remember my co-workers trying to give me orange juice. When I finally got to where I could think, I had orange juice all over me. It would be hours before I finally recovered from these episodes.

My mother and co-workers were very supportive and took good care of me. With time this happened less and less. I ate high protein foods and learned to eat even when I did not feel like eating. As I learned to handle stress better, eat better, and exercise more, these episodes happened only on rare occasions. My poor mother. The things I put her through.

I brought up low blood-sugars because they were triggered by stress and main stressor in those days was finances or the lack of them. The first years were the worst by far and I am glad that my mother was there during that first year because she had enough faith for both of us. It was an awesome feeling that I might not have enough money to buy food for my children or pay the rent. At first I did not have full-time work at the hospital and worked on call. Sometimes work was scarce because it was a small hospital.

My mother used to say, "Sarah, the Lord will not let you and your kids go hungry. He promised to meet all of your needs." I knew that she was right, but I had such a hard time believing. I often remembered the verse that said, "Consider the lilies of the field. They toil not, neither do they spin, yet Solomon in all his glory was not arrayed like one of these." I knew it was truth, but I had such a hard time, especially when the rent was due and I did not have the money. The truth is, we never went without food and the rent was always paid.

Impossible finances, the after-wash of divorce and a poor self-esteem were compounded in those first years. It is a wonder that we survive at all as individuals, never mind nurturing children who also experienced a divorce. But we do survive and we grow. Perhaps you do not believe as I do, that the needs will be met. I struggled with that belief even though I had been taught it as a child and knew that it was possible. My mother was by my side and she believed for both of us. You may not have a mother to encourage you and share her faith. For just a brief moment, let me be to you what my mother was to me and say, "Hold on tight. Trust. Your needs will be met."

Later I had a poster that said, "All I have seen teaches me to trust the Creator for all I have not seen." I can vouch for it. What I have seen in the past, tells me that all is well in the future.

The Hard Times
It's Cold in Dem Dar Hills

Actually, there were no hills, but it sure was cold, and the rain came down in buckets. I thought it rained a lot in Ireland, but the rain in Ireland ain't nothin' compared to the coast where we lived. When it rained hard, it sounded like thunder on the roof of our little trailer. Sometimes the wind blew the rain at a ninety degree angle and it felt like the trailer would blow away. In fact, sometimes I thought I would not have to put Henry's glue on the roof next year because there would not be a roof

The winters were cold and merciless. I have written many times about our wonderful wood-burning stove and it's warm glow. Well, this story is about the lack of warm glow, and is the opposite to happy evenings by the fireplace. You see, we also had gas, heat in our little home. Unfortunately, the gas heater was broken and I did not have the money to have it repaired.

I was working evening shift, which meant that I finished my shift at eleven-thirty P.M. The kids stayed with my friends each evening and I picked them up around eleven-thirty or midnight. It was winter and very cold. I remember each evening, quietly opening the door so that I would not waken my friends. My kids would be asleep on the couch. I had blankets in the car to keep the kids warm during the drive home.

First, I carried one kid to the car and covered him with a blanket. I'd hurry back in the rain and pick up the next kid trying not to let the rain soak her. I bundled the kids in the blanket and drove home in the rain and one at a time, carried them into the trailer and tucked them into their cold beds. The trailer was so cold, I could see my own breath. It was freezing cold and I would shiver.

Now, most of the time I was pretty wired after working a busy shift, so going to sleep immediately was out of the question. Lighting a fire would have been futile because it would take a while to heat up the trailer. The gas heater did not work and there was no television to watch. I used to be stiff with cold. Worse still, I was discouraged. I do not know why it affected me so negatively, but carrying the kids in the rain, putting them in cold beds, and sitting in the cold in the trailer really dis-heartened me.

I remember one such night, just crying because I was so cold and discouraged. I was just overwhelmed with despair and hopelessness. The rain poured down, the wind howled, and the children slept. I felt so all alone. Yes, I had friends, but I really was all alone and I was so cold. It makes me cold to even think about it. Did I cry every night? No. Did that feeling go away? No. Did I survive? Yes. But, that was a difficult time in my life. There was just something about going home to the cold and quiet that made me feel all alone.

By then, I was used to being alone, and I seldom felt lonely. But there was just something about going home to a cold trailer at midnight and carrying the kids in the rain that caused me to feel isolated.

Eventually, a light went on in my brain and it occurred to me to turn on the electric blanket, and go to bed and read. It felt good to snuggle down in bed with a book and know that the kids were safe in bed in the next room, but that gloomy, isolated feeling remained. I praised the Lord for all my blessings and prayed for a day-shift job. Soon, life would be back to normal.

A Small Heartache

I suppose it is possible to have a small heart-ache. A heart ache that doesn't make our heart break in two, but it still aches a little and causes us to be sad. Undoubtedly, we have all had them and will face more as we travel through life. It is a wonderful blessing that we cannot recall all the heartaches at the same time and relive them, or see into the future and experience, all at once, the accumulation of all the heartaches that lie ahead of us. We would probably die of broken hearts. Usually though, we do not die. We carry our little heartache until circumstances change or we heal.

I had a small heartache because I missed a small boy. He was around six or seven at the time; I believe he was in second grade. Once again, I was back on evening shift. The kids were being cared for by a friend who lived close by. Problem was, she did not want me to pick up the kids at midnight when the shift ended, so the kids spent the night at her home.

In the morning, I went to the babysitter's house to pick up Suzanne. My son had already left for school. Suzanne and I spent the morning together and then I took her back to the babysitter on my way to work. Unfortunately, I did not see Noah because he was only getting out of school at that time. This was our routine and it usually meant that I would not see Noah for four or five days at a time. Actually, each week it was a four or five day stretch.

Talk about missing someone. It was awful and my heart did ache for sure. I missed that happy little boy so much. Life just did not feel right when the three of us were not together. Going to the babysitter's house during working hours was O.K., but four and five day stretches were more than I could handle.

We do what we have to do. This is a true statement, but, Oh sometimes it is so difficult. Sometimes we do need to do things that cause our hearts to ache. This was a small heartache, and with time the circumstances changed. I remember other small heartaches similar to his one. I remember also, the bigger ones that felt as if my heart was going to break in two. It amazes me sometimes, how our poor old hearts survive the wear and tear of life here on Earth.

It amazes me also that some people have the courage to go on day after day. I looked upwards for help and healing. Without that help, I do not know how I would have survived. Perhaps, all the small heartaches in life would have broken my heart in two. Many times, I felt too tired to go on, and my heart was full of discouragement. I do not believe that I could have made it on my own strength. There were too many small heartaches, and He was the answer to every single one. Without the Lord's comfort, promises and healong touch, I could not have done it.

Christmas on the Beach

No, it wasn't Hawaii and it wasn't Mexico. It was the northern California coast. Rugged and untamed, it reminded me of some parts of the coast back home in Ireland. Cliffs, green grass, and frequent storms were somehow comforting. I love the ocean so much.

When I was twenty-one, I said farewell to family and friends in Ireland. I always had a restless spirit, I guess, and I chomped on the bit, anxious to see the big beautiful world. A team of wild horses could not have held me back. I was going and that was all there was to it.

And so, on August 16th, 1971, I boarded a ferry boat to Liverpool, where I would board "The Empress Of Canada" on one of her final cruises. I set out on a voyage which has lasted a lifetime. Little did I know then, that on my journey through life, I would sing and play many songs about leaving the shores of Ireland.

Little did I know how much that little Emerald Isle would be missed, and that possibly, never would the day arrive when I could go home to live there. If I had known what lay ahead, would I still have left?

Ireland is so small that no matter where we live, we are not far from the ocean. Actually, we are islanders. I knew that Canada was a huge country. I guess that I just had not thought about how far the east coast was from the west coast, and that in between there was so much land. Thousands of miles of land and no ocean. That was just too much land.

After I left home, it was thirteen months before I saw the ocean again along with a friend who was also from Ireland. We were so happy to see that big, beautiful ocean. It was a day I will remember for many more years.

Yes, the ocean is very special to me. The sound of the waves and sea-gulls. The colors of the setting sun, uniting sea and sky in a mass of color. It is magical and so good for the soul. It was good to move back to the coast. In fact it was better than good; it was wonderful.

There is a lot of rainfall and convection fog along the coast. Sometimes though, as the inland temperatures dropped, there were bright sunny days on the coast. It is hard to beat a crisp, sunny day by the ocean. The sky is so blue and reflects on the ocean. There were so many Christmas days just like this one. No rain. Just a beautiful crisp sunny day.

Time spent at the beach on Christmas day became a tradition while I lived on the coast. There is something about being alone on a family holiday. What a mixture of feelings all rolled together. How my thoughts and feelings churned sometimes on those trips alone to the beach on Christmas day.

Many times on Christmas Day, the kids were with their father and I usually ate dinner with friends. It is difficult to describe what I was feeling on those trips. I missed the kids. I knew they were safe, but it felt like we should all be together on Christmas Day. I missed my own family also. And as I sat on the rocks and looked around, I missed Ireland and cried deep in my heart because I knew that I could never leave the children, even when they were older and had children of their own. Suzanne used to say, "Mom, I want you to live beside me when I have kids". Yes this was my home now and this was my family.

Reality was that I could not even take the children to Ireland to visit, and that my little family would spend many Christmases away from home and a mom who loved them dearly. It was the plight of the immigrant, home, but never really home; and it was the plight of divorced parents whose kids were gone.

The waves churned the sand and beat on the rocks. Thoughts churned in my head and beat on my heart. There were no answers. The waves continue to rise and flow. I would continue to do the same. I shook the sand from my clothes and tried to shake any grain of self-pity from my heart. I would eat with my friends and be thankful for all the wonderful blessings in my life.

Chapter 8

A Time to Keep Silence, A Time to Speak

I have a favorite poet who wrote many years ago, "The Times They Are A'Changing." He wrote this about thirty years ago, and the times were changing. We were living Vietnam, Watergate, The Hippie Movement, riots in the streets, and in general, a revolution.

Yes, the times were changing then, and today they are changing even more. The economy is changing, and so is the Corporate World. Technology is changing rapidly, as evidenced by the Internet. We have advanced at an incredible pace.

Yet, with all of our achievements, we look around us and see that there is still violence and unrest, bigotry and discrimination. Violence and drug usage continues to increase and our prisons are packed to the max. The divorce rate continues to rise, as does the number of unwed mothers in spite of intervention.

Above all, we have witnessed a slow but sure decline of the family unit. More parents are raising children alone, more married mothers have needed to work to help pay the bills. As a result, more and more children are home alone without supervision. Believe me, I am not pointing the finger. This has been my own situation for many years now.

My mother did not work out of the home when I was a child. I used to waken up to a steamy bowl of porridge in the morning and ate it whether I wanted to or not. I was always hungry when I was a kid.

When we arrived home from school, it was too early for dinner, but there was always something good a 'cookin'. Mom did go out to work eventually. In fact, she went to nursing school. I don't remember being at a loss. However, when I was home in Ireland a couple of years ago, my younger sisters, now in their forties, said that they missed her a lot. They were old enough to take care of themselves, but they just missed those treats and the fact that she was not there.

When I left Ireland, I was not quite sure what divorce was all about. Now divorce in Ireland is common. I was not familiar with the word baby-sitter either. My dad was gone almost every night, but my mother was always home.

It may be erroneous thinking on my part, because I did not grow up here, but it seems that families stayed closer to home back in the day. Children had grandparents and even great-grandparents close by which meant a built in support system. Of course, there are families who still live close to one another, but it appears to me that it is not unusual for kids to have grandparents who live very far away. I know many single parents, like myself, who have no family close by.

Today, it is common for our kids to be cared for by someone who is not a family member. It is not uncommon for a child to have step siblings, and share the home with children of their parent's significant other. They may go and visit their other parent, and spend time not only with the other parent, but with his/her girlfriend/boyfriend, and his/her kids.

Sometimes a single parent needs to work two jobs to make ends meet, and the child spends even more hours away from home. Kids are very adaptable, and this is not the scenario for all kids, but it may be typical of life for many children in our country today.

Many children have to deal with so much up heaval in their lives today. Most of us, I venture to say, grew up with two parents, and even though there may have been some "ups and downs", our lives were quite secure. We had dinner at the same time every night, cooked by the same mom. When the kids were little, I cooked dinner every night. Over the last seven years, I often arrived home from work between seven and nine; sometimes even later. Suzanne spent many evenings alone and claimed that she did not mind, but it bothered me a lot.

She used to say, "I like being alone, in the evenings, but I don't like wakening up in an empty house." Many, many times she woke up in an empty house because I sometimes worked jobs which required leaving very early. I used to worry so much when I left her alone on those dark winter mornings, even if she was old enough to be alone.

Life is different for many children today. Life is different for many families today. I can only compare life for some children to the secure life I knew as a child, and that was typical of the family situations of the other kids I knew. I had aunts and uncles and we thought they were pretty cool. They had time for us and we looked up to them. I grew up in the country and neighbors and friends were hard-working farmers. And most of us went to the same church which was where a lot of our social activities took place. It was a fairly simple life, but it was safe.

Some children are alone after school until midnight when mom gets home from work. They live in a city where it is unsafe to go out. They have no family in town. Yes, our kids are adaptable, but this does not sound like fun and it cannot be a healthy situation.

And it seems to only be getting worse. More divorces. More single parents. More children from single parent families. More unplanned pregnancies. Where does it all end? What will be done?

Has our society even recognized that we are facing a real problem here? Once I went to a staff meeting at work when the kids were very young. Before the meeting the staff were chatting amongst themselves. Someone made a negative comment about the children from single parent families. I was offended and felt defensive of my own situation. I was upset that the assumption was that children from single parent families were the kids who ended up in trouble.

I disagreed because I knew that my own children were well loved, and I had great hopes for them, and knew that no matter what, I would always be there for them. We cannot assume that children from single parent homes receive less love, and will be neglected and allowed to roam the streets. I do believe though, that as the family unit declines in general, many more children spend time without supervision, and too much time alone, and it is a breeding ground for kids getting into trouble.

Many men today are "flaking out" on their responsibility of being the father of the house. Many men do not even pay "Child-support" for the children whom they helped conceive. Many women are choosing to leave children with a father while they pursue their own interests. I am not making rash judgments here. This is the culture we now know.

These scenarios have become quite typical, and many children are being deprived of the love and security which they deserve.

I remember when I was much younger, learning how children learn roles from parents. The little girl, looking up to her father, sees how the things that mom does for him please him so much, copies mom and does those little feminine things. A little boy, looking up to his dad, sees the things that dad does please mom a lot, copies dad, and learns things that a dad typically does.

Don't misunderstand me here. I think it is great that lots of men love to cook, and do things around the house. I think it is great that women today know how to work on their cars, and I wish I could work on mine. But what about those roles that children learn from parents? What about the roles children learn from both parents?

It almost broke my heart when my son went to live with his dad when he was twelve. I wanted to be part of his life as a teenager, yet I recognize that he learned a lot living with his father that he would not have learned living with me. I certainly could not have taught him about cars, and I would not have been able to be as firm as his father was.

Yes, our children are able to grow up satisfactorily with only one parent, but how much better off children could be with the love and provision of a mother and father. There are situations where a parent has such a negative effect on a child's life, that the child is better off growing up without the parent's influence in his life. I realize that a child is usually better off in a loving environment with only one parent, than to be subject to constant friction, and be exposed to emotional or physical abuse. Still, it makes me sad to see so many children grow up without the love and support of two parents.

Our culture is changing before our eyes. And what about the children from divorced homes? Will they follow our example and raise children alone? Where will it all end?

From Generation to Generation

My daughter loved her babies. Day after day, she and her babies reenacted every day scenarios in our own lives. She set the table and she and her babies ate dinner together. She took her babies shopping for groceries and prepared them for the babysitter's because she had to go to work.

One day, she asked if she could borrow the car (she was about five years old). I said that she could, and checked that the hand break was on tight. I continued to make dinner while she loaded the kids into the car. Each kid had his belongings packed and was wearing a seatbelt. She was so diligent and checked to see that all was in order. As I worked in the kitchen and listened to her talk to her kids and give advice about how they should behave, I thought to myself, "This must be a serious trip".

When the kids were all loaded in the car and seat-belts on, she said to me, "Mom, I will be back soon. I am taking the kids to their dad's to spend the weekend." My heart sank. I was so sad, because I realized then and there that she was only acting out what she saw in our own lives. After all, this was the life she knew. Mothers raise kids alone and take the kids to their dad's. This was her own life and this was normal.

Isn't this the "norm" for so many children today? To get a divorce and raise children alone? Today, divorce is rampant in our society. Do people really believe today that marriage is forever? Or do we marry today, thinking to ourselves, "Oh well, if it doesn't work out, I can always get a divorce".

I am only speaking here from my own experience. In the olden days, we usually went out with a guy because we had a crush on him (I don't know a better way to say that). We may not have thought consciously, "I'm gonna marry this guy, "but perhaps this was a given. I live in a small town and it seems like this is still the case. I do know though that the whole dating thing seems to have changed and I don't want to get into this because I don't know a lot about it.

The little that I do know (and I may be very wrong) is that dating is sometimes perceived as something that is not meant to last. Dating is important. It does not matter who we date, as long as we have someone to go out with (I'm talking about kids here). As I said before, I may be totally wrong. On the whole, what I see is possibly a lack of long term commitment. Is it any wonder that to many, marriage is not a lifetime commitment?

I am not saying that people are not sincere when they take their wedding vows, but that at the back of our minds we are already thinking, perhaps sub-consciously, that we will do our best and if it does not work, there is always divorce. Sometimes divorce is necessary, but regardless, it can cause devastation and pain.

Whatever children grow up with becomes normal to them. If dad hits mom because dinner is cold, that is normal to them. Scary, isn't it? Kids don't compare notes about what is normal in family life. They know only their own life and that is normal to them.

We do usually repeat in our adult lives what we knew when we were children. Children who have loving, caring parents usually grow up to become loving, caring parents. Children from divorced homes often become divorced adults. None of this is meant to be judgmental. I was married for only four years, so I am certainly not pointing a finger at anyone.

I share this only because I do believe that behaviors are passed from generation to generation. Abuse victims who die emotional deaths because of abuse, find themselves being abusive. The cycle has to stop somewhere. Today there is help available for those victims of abuse who despise their own abusive behavior.

We too, as single parents need to teach our children that it is not normal for children to grow up with only one parent. We can teach them that divorce is traumatic. Our children do not learn from our mistakes. All too often, they must learn from their own mistakes just as we did. I feel though, that there is a way. It is not fool-proof, but it gives me hope in this day and age. Children from single parent families can be taught about marriage.

They can be taught communication skills and taught how important communication is in a relationship. They can be encouraged to believe that marriage is a huge commitment and should be taken seriously. There is more to marriage than a fancy, wedding and a honey-moon. Marriage involves work and growth. They can be taught also that divorce hurts children and breaks up families. I believe that we can teach our children, even when they are young, that their decision about whom they will marry, is possibly the biggest decision they will ever make.

Maybe I am naive, but I do truly believe that if children were taught about marriage and knew what a commitment it really is, they might take it more seriously. Many of us did not have much choice about divorce, but I know that all over our country, there are children hurting as a result of it.

As a nurse, I have watched many people leave this world and I have seen many a loved one sit by the bedside and wait with hurting hearts.

One evening, an old man sat by the bedside of his dying wife. He held her hand and occasionally spoke quietly to her. I put my arm around him and he wept tears on my shoulder. He said, "She was my bride and I love her more today than I did on the day I married her".

He went on to tell me how she stayed with him during his drinking years. He said, "I was a hard man to live with, but she never left me. She stayed with me all those years and saw me through. She was a good woman". He had spent many years loving her after he quit drinking. Now he was here by her bedside.

I've seen many old people sit by the bedside of a spouse and speak lovingly of the one who was leaving. They sailed many rough seas together. They battled the storm together, "Till death does us part".

The old saying goes, "Behind every good man is a good woman". Behind every good woman is a good man. A bad marriage has wrecked many a good man or woman. We need to teach our children even while they are young, how important the marriage decision is. So few marriages survive these days, but my prayer is that neither of my children will ever experience divorce or raising children alone.

I pray that they will consider marriage the biggest decisions of their lives. I taught them while they were young. I pray that they will remember and not make the same mistake.

My Granny in Ireland

This morning I listened to an Irish tape. I was reluctant to listen to it, because it is almost Christmas and we Irish immigrants tend to become a little home-sick at Christmas. I listened to the tape and sang my heart out the whole hour as I drove to work. The songs were melancholy as those Irish songs tend to be, but I was moved and touched as I listened to the mandolin, flute and bag-pipes, and the guy's deep, rough Irish voice.

The tape has the most wonderful version of "I'll Take You home Again Kathleen" that I have ever heard. Tears flowed as I sang along. Kathleen's rosy Irish cheeks had faded since she left Ireland. In his deep Irish voice, he sang, "I'll take you home again Kathleen, to where your heart will feel no pain. And when the grass is fresh and green, I will take you to your home Kathleen". My heart was truly touched and I felt for the immigrants who left their homes in Ireland so long ago. It was different back then. Today, we save our money and return to our homeland. Back then, immigrants seldom made it back to their own country, and many died, dreaming of the life they knew as children.

Many immigrants have no home. They are glad to be here and have a better life, but in many ways, their heart is at home, and life will never be the same. I am more than happy to be here. My children are my family, and now I have lived here longer than I lived in Ireland. Still, I miss my family, and sometimes I miss Ireland. It is in my blood. It runs deep in my veins. I hear bagpipes and I am moved so deep in my heart that words cannot describe the feelings I experience. It is as if someone is stirring up a pot of soup, and I feel Ireland in my bones and in my very being. That does not mean that I am not happy with my life in California; it just means that Ireland is part of my very soul.

Anyway, another song on the tape was "Scarlet Ribbons". Many of you who are younger, will not know this song. It is an old song about a father who looked into his little girl's room one night as she was praying. She was saying, "And for me, some scarlet ribbons. Scarlet ribbons for my hair." The father goes out to try and find some scarlet ribbons for her hair, but alas, all the stores are closed and there are no scarlet ribbons. He sings, "Through the night, my heart was achin'",

Just before the dawn was breakin'
I peaked in, and on her bed,
In gay confusion, lying there,
Lovely ribbons, Scarlet ribbons,
Scarlet ribbons for her hair.

If I live to be two hundred,
I will never know from where,
Came those lovely Scarlet ribbons,
Scarlet ribbons for her hair.

It is a touching song, and it makes my head reel with nostalgia. You see, it is one of the songs that my grandmother used to sing to us when we were little children. I never quite understood the song and used to wonder where the ribbons came from, but I loved to listen to my Granny as she sang to us. We would gather round her and she would sing. It was a normal part of our lives. Sitting in front of the stove, listening to our own Granny sing. She would sing "Scarlet Ribbons," "Kevin Barry," "I'll Take You Home Again Kathleen" and many other songs. Many an evening we spent, listening to her sing. All of us sang. It was very much a part of our lives growing up.

She sang sad songs about life - about the two little orphan boys, and "I'm Nobody's Child", about a little blind orphan boy, whom no one wanted to adopt because he was blind. She used to sing a sweet little song,

> *Oh, yes my dear, there's something more,*
> *There's something more than gold.*
> *To know you're on your way to Heaven,*
> *To know your sins are all forgiven,*
> *Is something more than gold.*

It had an upbeat, happy tune to it, and many a time I find myself singing it as I work around the house.

My Granny is about ninety-five now and does not recognize her family. I went home last Christmas. In fact, it was tomorrow, a year ago, that I went home for the first time in seven years. My daughter and myself went to see Granny Bell. Her bed was in the living room and a big fire was burning, making the room so cozy, Granny was lying in the fetal position, snuggled under her quilt. How sweet she looked, like a little baby.

I helped her sit at the side of the bed, but she was tired and wanted to snuggle down under the quilt. She was so well cared for. Her skin was milky white, smooth and soft. She was in a world of her own and happy. Sometimes she talked to herself and then dozed off again. How sweet her world was, and how much love was given her by the daughters who cared for her. Suddenly, out of the blue, she started to sing. My daughter and I just smiled at each other. My daughter had worked with me during the summer. She had met the older folks I work with every day and had grown to love them. She knew that this was a happy, well cared for Granny, she did not sing for long, but my heart was touched. Even in her senility, she was singing.

About eight years before, when I took both kids home for the first time, she had been very entertaining. I was so excited to take my children to see the Granny who had been so special to me when I was a child. We all piled into the house and gathered around the fireplace because it was November and very cold. She was happy to see all of us, but not as happy as a Granny might be to see grandchildren from California for the first time. We had a good visit, considering the fact that she was deaf and a little senile. We had tea and treats. All of a sudden, she had a horror stricken look on her face. She looked like she had seen a ghost. I wondered what had happened, she said, "Sarah, (My mother's name is Sarah) there are two of them. "She was referring to my oldest sister and myself. Now, we do look alike, but all of the time, she had thought that I was Betty, just dropping by for a visit. We laughed hysterically and Noah and Suzanne thought it especially funny.

In spite of my Granny's deafness, my mother finally managed to convince her that Sarah was home from California and had brought the kids to visit. What a happy reunion it was after all. She was so happy to see us, even though she had been chatting to us for the last half-hour. During all of that time, she thought that I was my sister. It did not register with her until she saw my sister and I sit beside each other. It was a great visit, and it was a joy for me to introduce my children to her, even if she wasn't sure what was happening. The kids thought it was real funny and I have wonderful photographs of the kids with their great Granny in Ireland.

Yes, she was a great lady and I am glad that her daughters are caring for her. She deserves all the T.L.C. that this world can afford, because she was a hard working, wonderful lady. Her nickname was "Little Plum," because she was less than five feet tall and a little round. She wore an apron like the women in Ireland wore back in those days. I used to watch her comb her long hair, braid it on each side, then roll it into earphones on each side of her head.

Back then in Ireland, it was not unusual for Granny and Granda to come live with the family for a while. I do not know how that affected the adults, but it sure was a treat for us kids. My father's name for my Granny was "The battle ax". That kind of confused me at the time, even though he did call her that with humor and love, but back then I did not know anything about the dynamics between a mother and son-in-law.

I loved it when Granny and Granda stayed with us. It was like we had two moms. Granny was always busy in the kitchen and Granda was always working out in the garden. He was a great guy also and taught me so much. There was nothing that my Granda could not do. He was a quiet man, but when he spoke, we listened. He did not raise his voice and he was a peaceful man. We did not disobey Granda, and it was good to be around him. He loved to grow things and everything he touched was good. He loved to teach us how to do things. He was a bricklayer and finally died of emphysema, but before he died he taught me how to lay brick. Today, I could build a wall if I had to, or a fire-place (as long as it did not have too many fancy curves).

My Granda died about twenty-five years ago, and Little Plum was left alone. She missed him, even though they squabbled sometimes. They were good friends. Little Plum went on without him. On Sunday my mom called from Ireland.

Granny has a "Flu Bug" and it will be a miracle if she survives another winter. My Granny will be missed, but I still have all of those wonderful memories. My Granny made a difference in my life. Her singing, her love, and the wonderful example she showed us over the years. She used to say many times, "Count your blessings. "Granny, I count my blessings many times a day. I never laugh at those less fortunate than I am because you warned me many times never to do that. I see a man stagger in the street. I do not judge. Instead I say, "There but for the grace of God go I". You taught me all of this and I wish you were well enough to hear what I have to say to you. Better still, your reward is in Heaven, because you taught us so many great things.

I wish that every kid could have a Granny and Granda like mine. Before I left Ireland, I did not know what a babysitter was. My mother was home with us when we were little, and if and when she was not, Granny and Granda were there. Life has changed all over the world since then though, Life has changed much in Ireland also. When I left Ireland, I sort of knew what divorce was. I knew that for some obscure reason, a man and his wife were not together any more. Just before I left, I knew a couple that were sort of divorced because the guy had met a younger woman. It shocked the whole community.

I'm not saying that I am against divorce, because I believe that sometimes divorce is necessary, and over the years, many women have endured much. But over the years, on the whole, we have witnessed the family as a unit, fall apart in so many countries. Now in Ireland there are daycare centers, nursing homes and single parent families. I'm not judging single parents; I have been a single parent for sixteen years. I am not judging those of us who are divorced; I have been divorced sixteen years. Perhaps my childhood was unusual, but I doubt that. There are probably many, around the same age as myself who grew up with lots of love and wonderful grandparents. I would be crazy to say that there are not children who enjoy such a privilege today. I know many such families right here in this small town.

My perception on the whole though, is that this is not as common as it used to be. Many children live far away from their grandparents. Many children are divorced from their grandparents. Grandparents are very special people and it just seems to me that every kid could benefit from the special love that a grandparent provides so willingly. My mother loves her grandchildren. I wish that we had been closer so that my kids could have benefited from all the love she had to give them. I wish also that she could have been a bigger part of their lives.

The times, they are a changin'. I'm glad I lived in a time when Grannies and Grandas were part of a child's life. They taught me so much and shared so much of their lives without even trying. They were just there and part of the family. As a grandparent, I would not want to live with my children; they need to live their own lives. I do pray though, that I can be the Granny to their children that my Granny was to me. I hope I get to teach them many songs. I will teach them the songs that my Granny taught to me. I will sing "Scarlet Ribbons For Her Hair".

Chapter 9

A Time to Embrace, A Time to Refrain from Embracing

I know, without a shadow of a doubt, that I could probably give better advice about how to launch a spaceship, than I could about marriage, so believe me, this is not an attempt at advice on marriage. I am in my forties, and was married for only four years. Those four years were not good years in my life, and in fact, set me back instead of forward. The recovery time was much longer than the time spent in the marriage.

I believe in marriage, and believe that it is a good situation. Unfortunately, I've just never been brave enough to try it again. I came close to remarrying a few times, but something usually happened, and once again I was foot-loose and fancy free, as the saying goes. In retrospect though, I am so glad that plans fell apart, and the marriage did not take place. I am so happy to be single and I cannot even explain why. Yes, I have an idyllic dream that one day I will live by the ocean and write. I dream of having the freedom to come and go when I need or want to. I'm not opposed to doing any of it with the man I might meet, but somehow, it does not seem as important as it did before. When friends say, "But think of growing old alone," I find myself thinking, "I don't know what it is like to grow old". I will have to learn as I grow. But I do know what it is like to be alone, and usually I like that very much. Right now, I like being alone. I go out for coffee alone. I even go out for breakfast alone. I spend evenings alone, and weekends alone. For now, I like that. Perhaps I will change my mind later in life. Perhaps I will meet a guy whom I would be happy to share my life with, I'm not opposed to that. The important thing is that there is no need or urgency. I have learned to be happy alone. I do not need another individual to make me happy. I am happy and content with my life.

I share this for a very good reason. As a single mother with two little children, I did not always experience the peace and contentment I experience now as a single person. I realized that I needed to experience a lot of growing and healing, and that I needed to find peace and contentment in my own heart without depending on another individual to make me happy. I knew that I was not ready for another relationship until I had totally healed and found happiness within. I realized that there was no knight in shining armor, riding a white stallion, who would sweep down and rescue me and make everything all right. I knew all of this, but I was human and needy. Always in the back of my mind, I believe, was the hope that one day, I would meet a wonderful man. A very special man.

I do not put myself down for this. It is a natural thing which we all experience. Isn't it the hope in most of our hearts that we will meet that special someone? I believe it is. As children, we played with our dolls and we played house. Ask little girls what they want to do when they grow up, and many times you will be told, "I'm gonna get married and have babies." Most of us want to be with that special someone. We want to share our lives with that "someone" and have children. Most men want to go home at the end of a busy day and be with their families. Most women want to be with a special person and be part of a family. I realize that I am making generalizations. There are exceptions for sure, especially after we have been hurt or rejected, but I do believe that most of us want to be part of a family. Yes, it is probably very normal to want to be with our special partner, but sometimes it's this wanting so much to be with a special person that gets us into so much trouble, especially as single parents. This longing is further complicated by need and loneliness.

Vulnerable

Most of us want to be with that special someone. No matter how successful we are, or how rich our lives are, most of us want that special someone to share with. There are people who are successful and rich, yet they do not have that "special other person" in their life, and they are lonely. None of us are an island. There is a deep need to share our lives with another individual.

To meet that "special other' is a need in most of our hearts, and it starts when we are very young. That special other not only will meet all of our romantic needs, but will be our best friend and love us for "who" and "what" we are.

This need to meet that "special other" motivates us from an early age. It is as real as the need to eat and drink. Unfortunately, for single mothers, especially after the recovery period, that need can, be double trouble. Our need to meet a significant other is compounded by our loneliness, and neediness.

Yes, we have got our act back together, and we are ready for another relationship. We made a mistake the first time, but that was because we were too young, we got pregnant, we did not know what we wanted.

Now in our search, we may be doubly needy. We struggle financially and rush hither and thither to work and the babysitter's. We have a difficult time making ends meet, and pray for a miracle before every payday. There is little or no money to socialize much, and no money left to pay for babysitting if we did want to go out.

Anyway, we want to spend time with the kids. We are lonely, and we are tired, we wish we had a "special someone" to share the load, and with whom we could share our hearts. A special someone to share the couch with and watch a good movie. A special someone to snuggle up in bed with.

Yes, life could be very different with someone to share our lives and burdens with. Are we vulnerable? I think so! Vulnerable is probably an understatement. Sometimes the loneliness is profound. Because, we are all alone. Yes, we have friends who love and support us. They go home to their husbands. We lie in bed alone, and yes, we feel alone.

We go to bed alone night after night. We ponder over the events of the day. We plan tomorrow. This might be common practice for many singles all across America, but for single parents, it may be especially awesome. Single people may go out on a Friday night and make the most of being single. Single parents usually stay home with the kids. The difference is not just the freedom to go out on a Friday night, but the awesome responsibility facing the single parent.

Yes, we are vulnerable, and we sometimes experience profound loneliness that words don't readily describe. Perhaps I am the only single mom who felt like this occasionally, but I doubt that this is so. Maybe I felt it because I had not felt that closeness and togetherness for many years with another individual.

Being a single parent is far from easy, and there are times when we might despair. It is natural to want to share our lives with a "special someone," but I think that we need to be cautious and not be blinded by our need. Sometimes we cannot see the forest for the trees. Worse still, some of us might choose not to see.

Queen of Denial

Me, a queen? I live in blue jeans and flannel shirts. I love to ride horses, work in the yard, and grow beautiful flowers. I seldom dress up, even though I have nice clothes hanging in the closet. Glamorous I was not. Queen, I was.

I was the Queen of Denial. This is not a put-down to myself. We all do it to a greater or lesser degree, even the healthiest of us. Even though it was not funny at the time, and is still not funny, I have learned so much. Years later, I still fall into "denial". Now, when I do this, I am hit between the eyeballs with a ton of bricks. It bowls me over and I can laugh at myself.

I hope never to lose the compassion I have. My life would be empty without compassion and love. But, when I start making excuses for a man in my life, or find myself denying truth that is obvious, I immediately recognize my own Denial.

I don't just deal with "denial" in relationships, but in many aspects of my life. Truth staring me in the face, I choose to believe that what I see is not real. It hurts less to put reality aside and believe what we choose to believe.

Denial is real. We do it in an attempt to reach our comfort zone. Not being in a state of "denial" means facing the truth and making decisions that we sometimes do not want to make. We may see all the signs that our child is using drugs. We see the difference in his/her personality. We see the irritability, the sudden drop in grades, and the failure to follow through with things. How many of our children have traveled down this road alone, and we could not face the stark reality?

A common situation for even very healthy people, is when a marriage starts to fall apart. Couples often rationalize and say that they are not as close because of "busyness" with kids and work. Reality says, often loud and clear, "We are drifting apart". Denial says, "Oh, we are just busy and tired, it will get better". Couples who face reality acknowledge problems, deal with them, and the marriage may be saved.

Couples, usually one more than the other, say, "Oh, this is just a rough spot, it will go away". Most of us know though, that issues not dealt with do not go away. Issues grow. Unforgiveness and resentment fester like a cancer. We make it look like it is working on the outside, when on the inside, the fire is going out, and unfortunately may reach the point where it can never be rekindled without divine intervention.

I say "Queen of Denial", because when it came to denial, I won the prize. I'm not putting myself down, only acknowledging a truth. You see, sometimes, we have such great hopes. Hope is a strong motivating force and it is good to have hope. It is good to expect wonderful things to happen in our lives.

Trouble is, sometimes, we have such great hopes and expectations that we unknowingly control and try to make something work, even when it is destined to fail. The red lights are flashing! Danger signals are alerting us, but we want something so much that we choose not to see what we perceive. Our best friends might be concerned and bravely approach us. Our inner heart tells us not to proceed. In our denial, we choose to proceed anyway. Maybe you are much smarter than I was. I hope so!

Actually, smart is probably a poor choice of a word in this instance. Denial does not have a lot to do with smartness or intelligence. Perhaps this is the scary thing about denial. Ever notice how even the smartest, most intelligent, and successful people can really lose it in a relationship? All common sense appears to make a nosedive out of the window. All of their friends are saying, "You're nuts, can't you see?"

Fact is, they, we, do not see. We are infatuated. Infatuated by an ideal. Infatuated by what that person is and could be with our love. Yes, he has a tendency to drink too much, or spend money foolishly, or has a problem holding down a job. Yes, he does have some problems, and he doesn't really care much for kids, but with a love like ours, all of that can change. Ever find yourself thinking like that?

Ever find yourself making excuses for your significant other? I did, and probably to a shocking degree. Not necessarily these examples, but I did make excuses and try to make it work, when it was obvious to others that it was a hopeless situation.

Do I still experience Denial? Yes, I do. I accept that this was probably a defense mechanism which I used during most of my life. The good news is, it doesn't cause as much grief in my life any more, as it did in the past. I still want to accept people. I want to understand people, but I don't have to deny what is truth! I think what helped the most was striving to understand myself. My heart is often filled with love, but do I always love everyone around me? Certainly not always. In my heart, I am a loving person, and often reach out with love. Are my actions always loving? Unfortunately, many of my actions, thoughts and reactions are far from loving. I don't like the times when I am unloving or indifferent. At these times, I feel a real lack of peace. Sometimes I like the person I am growing to be. Often I do not like my behavior.

Most of all, I am learning to accept myself - the strengths and weaknesses. The exciting part of all of this is, that while I recognize my many weaknesses, come to terms with them, and determine to change and grow, I am more aware that there are other caring people going through the same thing.

As I learn to love myself, with all of my strengths and weaknesses, I can more readily love and accept those around me. As I learn to love my imperfect self, I also learn to love the many imperfect others around me. And what this all means, is that I can love and accept people around me for who they are and in spite of their faults. I don't have to focus on all the wonderful things about them and deny the obvious shortcomings.

How does this change anything? It changes a lot of things. Best of all, it means that I can make choices. I don't have to be totally infatuated with someone, so that I can only see the Wows and deny what might be obvious shortcomings. Now hopefully, I can realistically meet someone, recognize characteristics I like, and characteristics I don't like, and make rational decisions up front. Can I live with this?

This all takes away the need of denial and helps me to make healthy choices. And it doesn't just apply to romantic relationships, but to work relationships also.

As single parents, we may be very vulnerable. We are doing alone what is often difficult for two parents who love each other to do together. We are the soul breadwinner, and mom and dad, all rolled into one. It is not unusual or surprising that we would want a special other person to be close to and share our lives with.

It is understandable that in our aloneness and our need of companionship, that we might deny or ignore the flashing Red lights or the vivid signs that say, "Do Not Proceed!" It is all understandable. Nonetheless, the results may be disastrous if we choose not to heed the warnings, and deny what we are perceiving. You may have been through one divorce already and it wasn't an easy road. Being in Denial and ignoring the flashing Red Lights may well lead to another painful divorce.

Watch out for denial and recognize it for what it is. You may be tired and you may be lonely. Question is, "Are you better off, tired and lonely, raising your kids in a loving environment, or locked into a miserable marriage with conflict, born out of need?"

Look before You Leap

You'd better look before you leap
Still waters run deep
And there won't always be someone there
To pull you out.
And you know what I'm talking about.
I never promised you a Rose Garden.

There is no Rose Garden.

Much can be said about marriage and many books have been written on the subject. Probably, we have all heard, "Love (marriage) makes the world go around." Personally, I believe in marriage. It was ordained by God, and was meant to be a blessing. There is a wonderful story in the beginning of the Bible about marriage. God created Adam in the Garden of Eden, a wonderful and beautiful place that many of us might dream about escaping to. This place was Paradise. God also created the animals and Adam named them, one by one

Soon, God saw though, that in spite of the beautiful Garden and all of the animals, there was not a suitable friend for Adam, and that he was lonely. Now, God loved Adam, His very own Creation, and blessed him with a special friend and companion. Adam and Eve were very happy as they played in the Garden. Adam was not lonely anymore. He had a wife.

Marriage is a very special relationship. A bond ordained by the One who created us. You may not believe any of this, but I think most of us will agree that there is a deep need in most of us to be with a special partner. I know people who are happily married and choose daily to stay together. They have a good relationship, but I don't think they would call the relationship a "Rose Garden." Maybe they would.

In many ways, marriage is like a garden. I love to garden and I especially love to grow flowers. Every summer I spend many enjoyable hours working in the yard. Gardens don't just happen. They require planning, fertilizing, planting, watering, cultivating, weeding and yes, even replanting. Marriage, like gardening needs a lot of love and attention. It takes a lot of work, especially weeding and nurturing. It takes energy, dedication and honesty.

A well cared for marriage can be a blessing just like a beautiful garden in full bloom. A bad marriage on the other hand can be traumatic and devastating. In a neglected garden, the weeds grow and smother the flowers. The ground becomes dry and hard, and flowers cannot grow. There is no water for growth and the flowers finally die.

As singles, we often long for marriage. Of course, we want the marriage symbolized by the beautiful garden. If we marry the wrong person, out of need or desperation, we could end up with the marriage symbolized by the neglected garden.

I cannot speak for others here, I can only speak for myself. I would rather be a single plant with water and sunshine, and be alone, than be a flower strangled by weeds and eventually die from lack of water. I'm not suggesting that single parents should not remarry. Marriage was meant to be wonderful, and can be so. I just fear for those who marry out of need, and find themselves in a bad marriage again, a dying strangulated flower.

Be Not Weary in Well-Doing

Once I had a male friend who really wanted to get married. I was not at all interested in marrying this person. Aside from not being attracted to the person, I saw major problems. He made a lot of money and had a lot to offer. He really loved to be around the kids.

I shared this with a friend who was older and very pragmatic. I was astounded at her response. "Sarah, you can't keep doing this. You have two children to raise and this man has a lot to offer you. What is wrong with you?" I was flabber-ghasted! I used to care so much about the advice friends had to offer. The admonition threw me into a tizzy. (I can laugh at myself now). I struggled with the rebuke. Am I supposed to marry someone just because he offers financial security? What about love, togetherness, sharing and common goals?

Of course, I made my own decision. I could have financial security and be very unhappy, or I could continue to struggle as a single mom, living in a happy loving home with happy loving children. Believe me, I have no regrets. I am glad that I made my own decision. More than once I was offered financial security in the form of marriage. Believe me, I still struggle sometimes, but I am still glad that none of these marriages came to pass.

Well-meaning friends counseled me, "Sarah, you are looking for a perfect marriage and there is no such thing." Perhaps they were correct. I wasn't looking for a perfect marriage I wanted a good marriage. A good marriage has its ups and downs, trials and problems to be solved. A bad marriage is a nightmare.

As you recover from your divorce, you may anticipate and look forward to another marriage. That is normal, I believe, because most of us do want to share our lives with a special friend. This time, be aware and smart. Don't rush in where angels fear to tread. Treasure that dream and be patient. I'm sure a good marriage is worth waiting for. Don't marry out of need.

If your next marriage fails, who will be there to pull you out?

Who will be there to pull you out?

Perhaps you breezed through your divorce and went on about your life. I didn't. I found myself in a country, miles from home, and two tiny children to raise. My self-esteem was rock-bottom, and my confidence had dwindled to nothing. I had made a terrible mistake, and now

I had to start from scratch and put all of the pieces back together. Had I left without the scars and wounds, it would have been much easier. However, the wounds were there, and the scars ran deep. I had consciously taken a wrong turn and it ended in disaster.

I was glad to leave and eagerly turned the page to a new chapter in my life. It was a new beginning, and I was more than ready for the change. Although we might be relieved to leave a bad marriage, many of us are negatively affected by the fact that the life we had hoped for, will not be a reality. Instead of our children living with the two parents who love them, they will live with only one parent. Many of us feel that we have failed, we face a tremendous undertaking, and because of circumstances in the relationship, we suffer from low self-esteem. This is not a truth for all of us who are single parents, but it is reality for many of us.

Often in a marriage turning sour, individuals have a need to tear down the other person, and hurtful things are said. In our pain and disappointment, we rip each other apart. Is it any wonder that we separate with our self-esteem on the ground? The reality of divorce is bad enough. Add to it, the bitterness and anger, and we are often left with two individuals who feel very bad.

Our self-esteem is a terrible thing to lose. We lose our worth and the ability to value ourselves as individuals. In our own eyes, we are not worthy of love. We are not lovable.

If one failed marriage can produce such crippling feelings, and we survive and regain our self-esteem, how devastating the second divorce must feel if it occurs under similar circumstances. Who will be there to pull us out of another divorce? Our self-esteem is precious. I once lost mine and it was a dying experience.

I have learned that when we lose our self-esteem, we lose everything. I am not talking about "ego" here, I am talking about our own self-worth. Self-esteem is about how we value ourselves as human beings. Yes, "we may value other people, and give them the respect they deserve. Question is, do we love and respect ourselves? The Lord does.

Perhaps you were told in a bad relationship, or even as a child, that you were stupid and ugly; that you were unlovable. Sound as our self-esteem may have been at one point, constant recitals of how hopeless we are often penetrate our subconscious until we finally do believe that we are unlovable and a total failure.

Today, I believe in myself. I do not always like my actions or my behavior, but I like who I am, and I like who I am becoming. I believe that I am lovable and I certainly believe that I am loved. I believe that I have a lot to offer, and that I am capable of doing wonderful things in this lifetime. Now, I am confident and bold. I believe that good things have happened and will continue to happen in my life. I expect good things to happen. I know also that I will have the grace and courage to face the trials that come my way.

For a while in my life, I lost my self-esteem, and I share all of this for a reason. It took years to recover what was once so naturally mine, but I learned an incredible lesson. Now, I guard my self-esteem like it is gold. Yes, I may need to deal with abusive people who have a need to tear down other people. However, I will not voluntarily subject myself to them. I remove myself graciously.

If your self-esteem rock-bottomed as mine did post-divorce, how-will it survive a second trauma? I'm not suggesting for a second that you never remarry. I am suggesting that you be patient and hang in there until you are very sure that this is the person with whom you want to spend the rest of your life. Don't, out of need, jump from the frying pan, into the pot. Will this new relationship tear you down or build you up? Don't traumatize yourself and your sweet kids. Hang tight and don't settle for second-best.

You Are Wonderful
Don't Settle For Second Best

Not everyone who experiences divorce has a low self-esteem. Some go into a marriage with a low self-esteem. Some folks even experience more than one divorce with self-esteem intact and faring well.

I want to share with those whose self-esteem, for whatever reason, is frail and somewhat shattered. When we have a good self-image, and value our lives, we usually treat people well and expect the same in return. We expect to be treated well and that is usually what happens when we feel deep down that we are worthy of other peoples' love and respect. What happens in our lives when we see ourselves as failures; unlovable and "bad?" What often happens is that unpleasant things do come into our lives. Fact is, unpleasant things come into most people's lives. Problem is, if your self-esteem is low, you will probably accept the unpleasant as a way of life, and figure that somehow you deserve this.

If, on the other hand, you were confident about who you were, did not feel powerless and deserving of "bad" things, you would believe enough in yourself to take charge and change the unpleasant, knowing that you are valuable.

To someone who is truly hurting, whose life is on the rocks, these may sound like a bunch of empty words. I want to tell you though, that I once hurt and felt so unlovable. I had nothing left inside. My confidence was gone. I wasn't even me anymore. In the past, I had traveled a lot, played my guitar and sang in front of people, gone new places and fitted in without problem. I had reached the point though where I did not have much faith in myself.

I do not want to dwell on this much, because it is not the case anymore. I know that this is an extreme case, that most of you who read this book may never have felt like this and I pray that you never do. However, I share it for a couple of reasons, the main one of course being that which fits this topic. How we feel inside about ourselves is what attracts certain people into our lives. Did you ever say to yourself or to a friend, "How do I meet these kind of men?" Sound familiar?

Once at an Easter gathering, I met a woman about my own age and we started chatting. She was a real extrovert, loved to chat and we later became great friends. Out of the blue, she asked me a poignant question "Did you ever ask yourself why patterns repeat in your life?" I was a little taken a back because I had never recognized a pattern in my life. I gave that question a lot of thought and set about to find out some answers over the next few years.

One surprising truth that unfolded, was that not only do we attract a certain type of person, depending on how we perceive our own self-worth, but that we will often be treated in a relationship exactly how we expect to be treated. This is important. If you have a good self-esteem, and a guy starts to not treat you well, it's good-bye Charlie, isn't it? You know how you want to be treated by a man, and this is not what you had in mind. (I'm not talking about marriage here).

On the other hand, if your self-esteem is not very good, and some guy starts to not treat you well, you might stay longer. After all, you are not real pretty, and you are not especially lovable. Better to have some love than no love at all. And, maybe you do not deserve any better.

For me, relationships changed drastically over the years. You'd think to hear me, I had a hundred or so. I didn't. But in seventeen years, I've bumped into some very nice men. What I want to share with you, is that as I changed, so did the men I attracted into my life. As my self-esteem recovered, and I really started to feel good about who I was inside, I met kinder men who cared a lot and treated me very well. In fact, they treated me like a princess.

I believe that each individual is very special. We all deserve to be treated with love and respect. Don't settle for second best. There are a lot of good men who know how to treat a woman well. Don't rush into something because you think you may not have another opportunity. If your self-esteem is on the low side, be patient and take time out to work on it. Recognize your strengths, and work on the weaknesses. Work on learning to love yourself and grow to love yourself as the wonderful, special person you are. It takes time. Make choices to not be around someone who tears you down and belittles you.

As your confidence grows, you will probably find that you attract different people into your life. As you learn to treat yourself well, you will probably find that others treat you well also. And, as you learn to take charge and change the negative things, which come into your life, you will expect good things to happen.

Above all, YOU ARE WONDERFUL. Don't settle for second best.

CPSIA information can be obtained
at www.ICGtesting.com
Printed in the USA
FSOW01n1133101115
13192FS